T. L. Scott

TLS Publishing

<u>Also by T. L. Scott</u>

<u>The Scary Picture Book Series</u>

A Scary Story

Ride With The Wind (A Scary Story)

A Fairy Good Night (A Scary Story)

<u>The Bill Thompson Thriller Series</u>

Fault Line

Shifting Sands

<u>The Reality Jumper Series</u>

Levels

Tunnels

T. L. Scott

Things I Wish I Knew

When I Stood

Where You Are Now

Things I Wish I Knew

When I Stood

Where You Are Now

T. L. Scott

TLS Publishing

2026

Editor - Lia Ottaviano

Cover Art - Kristen Andrews

Table of Contents

Introduction

Are you looking for a book with all the answers? Answers to questions you haven't even thought to ask yet? Sorry, this isn't that book.

I love writing fiction stories. I have written five novels and two children's picture book series so far. Maybe you've read some of my books. Maybe this is the first time you have come across my work.

In each of my stories, I love getting to know the characters and the settings they inhabit. As much as the stories are works of fiction, parts of me, my life experiences, find their way into the story. They weave the tapestry that binds the setting, characters, and plot together. In many ways, the stories are a reflection of me and the accumulation of what has transpired in my world. These pieces of me come out in various ways and become a part of these fictional tales. Some are subtle brushes with what I have experienced, while others are more directly related to my actual life experiences and lessons.

This book, *Things I Wish I Knew When I Stood Where You Are Now,* is no different. It is a representation of me. This time, I stand in front of the curtain. I am letting you into my world, my life. I am sharing the things I wish I'd known along the way.

The lessons in this book are ones I wish I had been taught much earlier in life. Hopefully, you will avoid some of my missteps and pitfalls. I hope you avoid some of my worst face plants and the inherent pain those errors brought me. It is with that intention that I pass these lessons on to you.

Some lessons have been passed down to me by people I have great respect for. I had some really good teachers along my way. I remember my sixth-grade teacher, Mr. Parish, giving me some advice I really needed at the time. At that age, kids are trying to figure out how they fit in. I was no exception. I was a new student at the school that year. He simply told me to be myself. He told me not to try so hard to impress others. Just concentrate on being the best version of yourself. That was very sound advice. I learned to embrace it more and more as the years went on. I have passed that wisdom down to my own children.

Fitting in has never been easy. I believe it is even more difficult now. Our sphere of influence has expanded from our local bubble of peers to include the worldwide community. Along with that widened scope comes increased pressure to keep up and somehow fit into the latest trends. Let it go. As individuals, you, me, and all of us are different by definition. Embrace that difference. Simply concentrate on being the best version of yourself. Become the very best you that you can be.

I had fantastic mentors during my time in the Navy. Leaders who were strong and steady. Leaders who communicated what they wanted and then followed up to see how it was going.

They would take advantage of those moments to train me on the challenges I was encountering, respond to my questions, listen to my recommendations, and provide constructive feedback. Those leaders were steady. I knew where they were coming from. I knew I could have open communication with them. This is not to say they were always easy to get along with. They were demanding in their expectations. It was those expectations that set the example of always striving to improve. To always try to do and be better.

Other lessons came from those whom I decidedly do not respect. There were also those people in leadership positions who were primarily out for themselves. They would take credit for what others had done. They did not seek input from others. They saw it as a challenge to their authority. By doing so, they shut down that open path of communication.

They also shut down avenues of innovation. Needless to say, the environment was not healthy.

People are people, and you will see all types along your journey. I know I have. At this point in my life journey, I can clearly see the value in both types of lessons.

Therein lies a constant truth in all our lives. We learn as we go. We learn from the good as well as the bad. We learn from our successes and arguably, even more so, from our almost wins and our complete and utter failures (face plants).

We enter this world as relatively blank slates. There are schools of thought that believe we come into this world with basic knowledge "hardwired" from the start. One example that addresses this is the instinct theory.

The instinct theory of motivation was derived from the studies of Charles Darwin. The theory evolved over the years and was further refined by William McDougall with his Instinct Theory of Motivation. Basically, instinct theory is what we already know. When mammals are born, we instinctively gasp for our first breath. Mammals seek to suckle from their mother. Baby chicks turn their heads toward the sound of their mother returning to the nest and open their beaks to receive food. Sea turtles head to the sea upon emerging from their egg.

We observe many more examples of instinctual activities in the animal world, as well as among our fellow humans. We know these things prior to our demonstration of instincts. They are universal. How does this happen? How do we know what to do? Studies have evolved over the years, influenced by Charles Darwin, Sigmund Freud, and William McDougall.

McDougall identified 18 distinct instincts, including curiosity, laughter, food-seeking, and reproductive behaviors. He proposed that these behaviors are passed down to increase survivability.

I don't want to get off topic here. I just want to make an example—a very simple one. What we call instinct is, in fact, behaviors passed on to us. These are basic instincts, for lack of a better term.

We have a natural respect for falling from great heights. Well, most of us do. Most of us also have an aversion to spiders and snakes. We possess some basic knowledge. Knowledge that we accept as truth. These fundamental truths may, in fact, be passed down through generations.

Things I Wish I Knew When I Stood Where You Are Now

For some of us, our family shares their knowledge with us in many ways. We help out around the house and are praised when we do well and scolded when we do not. That said, not all of us were raised by family members who praised us. Some of us had far more severe discipline than being scolded. Even in these harsh environments, we learn. We learn what not to do as well as how best to avoid those harsh consequences.

We are always learning. We inherit this knowledge because it has helped us survive, even thrive, in the face of adversity.

Most of humanity has evolved. We no longer live in small, isolated communities. We live in a much larger and close-knit society. This society is connected through transportation hubs, including highways, railways, airports, and the internet, the information superhighway.

Our news feeds provide information on a global scale in near real time. Not so long ago, really a small fraction of our existence as humans, we received nearly all our communication through human interaction, people telling each other what they knew.

In 1844, Samuel Morse sent the first message from Washington, DC, to Baltimore. In 1845, the Magnetic Telegraph Company launched the first commercial line from Washington, DC, to Baltimore. This sparked a rapid expansion of telegraph lines across America. The telegraph was expanded in stages. The eastern part of the country, where most of the population resided, was first to be developed. The telegraph spread west to the Mississippi River as the waves of settlement spread. The final area was the vast American West. It was sparsely populated, with the exception of California.

The Pony Express was the answer to the telegraph for the West. As the railroads expanded, so too did the telegraph lines. The Pony Express marked a significant leap forward in communication. It significantly cut down the time between correspondence for people spread out over vast distances.

As wonderful as the Pony Express was, it was very short-lived, lasting from 1860 to 1861.   Messages that had taken months to reach recipients now took mere moments. Prior to this advancement, the fastest form of communication across the vast distances of the American West was the Pony Express. The cause of its demise was the rollout of the telegraph throughout the West. The ponies could not outrun those signals.

Innovations in communication have continued to evolve into what we currently take for granted. We walk around with telephones that can make calls to virtually anywhere in the world, as long as the person at the other end has an active phone.

These communication devices, commonly referred to as smartphones, are equipped with internet access. These smart devices enable us to access a vast collection of knowledge on a scale never before seen. This collective knowledge is accessible to a large portion of humanity worldwide.

Ah, here we are. I told you that I would make my point. It is this knowledge, this access to knowledge, that I want to focus on.

Now, imagine for a moment the sheer power of having access to this knowledge. If we enter this world with basic instincts and a fundamental understanding of how the world works, we are equipped with the knowledge necessary for survival and awareness of how it operates at a fundamental level. We take it for granted, but it is incredible. Now, imagine if that level of knowledge were expanded in line with the increased accessibility to knowledge about our world.

Compare that access to knowledge to when Plato and Descartes pondered their weighty thoughts. What if they had had access to the collective libraries of their time without having to travel there in person? Imagine if they were able to collaborate with their scholarly peers in real time, rather than via hand-delivered letters that took months or longer to arrive.

Very few people knew how to read and write. Books were rare commodities. They were expensive to create and costly to transport. How many potential geniuses were not afforded the opportunity to realize their potential because they were occupied with the very real struggle to survive? There wasn't much time to ponder questions weightier than how you were going to survive the next few days and provide for your family.

In this day and age, we are more fortunate than we realize. We take our technology for granted. We need to appreciate the great gift we have been afforded and take advantage of this opportunity.

Ask questions and seek out the answers. Ask how things work. Ask why things are the way they are. Learn! Don't simply rely on your search engine to get the answer, or use AI to provide a summary. Dig deeper into the information. Learn the how, not just the what, of things. Increase your knowledge.

Let's make this endeavor of passing down knowledge an intentional one. I hope you will continue to join me on this journey. It has taken me 55 years (and then some) to get to this point. It is my sincere hope that by sharing with you the lessons, experiences, and wisdom I have attained along my journey, you, yes you, will stumble fewer times, wander less astray, and hopefully achieve a greater level of success, however you choose to measure it.

I suppose it is only fitting that I share my own journey with you. That is what this is all about, right? How can I assume to pass down the drops of wisdom I have gleaned throughout my life without sharing some of that life with you? I cannot do that in good faith.

So, here we go. I grew up in a rather large family. Five kids make for an interesting mix: four boys and one girl. My parents were very regular. Yes, they were basically normal in every way. I am referring to their regularity in bringing us children into the world.

Every two years, a child was born except for one gap. I learned later that this was due to an unfortunate miscarriage. After this tragic event, things returned to relative normalcy, and two years later, our sister arrived. Her arrival was very welcome after three boys in a row.

My parents had achieved their goal of having children. They had their boys and the coveted daughter. Life had a surprise in store, though. Right on schedule, my baby brother arrived. Let me explain further about just how regular my parents were. Every one of us boys was born in March. Our dear sister was not very far from that window. She came into our lives in April. Yes, you see it now, I bet. My parents were very regular.

Life was good. Dad had a good job, and as was normal for that time, from the late 60s through the mid-70s, Mom stayed at home and took care of the house and all of us kids. I think she had the most demanding job.

I have very fond memories of my younger years. We played with each other and the other kids in the neighborhood. We played outside and went wherever we wanted. We jumped our bikes off homemade ramps and rode those bikes down stairs at the local school and parks. We engaged in play battles. Explored the woods and streams. We had dogs. We had cats. We had a good life. Life, oh, you grand trickster. You had surprises in store for us. We couldn't have known at that idyllic time that my life, my siblings' lives, our family was going to blow up.

My father was a salesman, and his job required him to work long hours. Sometimes he had to stay overnight in hotels to continue his sales route. Something made my mother suspicious.

I have clear memories of my mom packing us into the car—a station wagon with plenty of room for all five children and, in better times, two loving parents.

Things I Wish I Knew When I Stood Where You Are Now

My mother turned into a stalker. Her late-night searches led us to motel after motel. We traveled many miles on many nights, crisscrossing my father's sales routes across the Midwest. I recall one epic fight my parents had in a motel parking lot.

Her suspicions had been confirmed. As a sleepy-headed child, I had no idea what was happening. All I knew was that it was strange. I was scared to see my parents fighting. They had argued before, but it was nothing like this.

My mother was screaming at my father and hitting him in the chest. My father was doing his best to ward off her blows while yelling back at her to be quiet. I remember other adults breaking them apart.

The drive home was horrible. I remember thinking that it lasted for a very long time. I kept waking up to hear my mom crying. She had the radio on, but I could still hear her sobs.

The next significant event I remember was the final fight between my parents. I am sure they had other small skirmishes, but this one was the final battle. I woke up to the sound of their raised voices. I snuck down the front stairs as quietly as I could. I wish I hadn't. I wish I had just stayed in bed. I was too curious and just had to see.

From my vantage point, midway down the stairs, I saw my mother on her knees begging my dad to stay. Her hand gripped his pants. She begged him to choose his kids over his lover. She didn't beg him to stay for her. She begged him to stay for us.

He pulled away from her. I remember clearly how she looked as he walked away. She was on her knees. She watched him walk into the kitchen and then out the door. She dropped her head. Her back bent. She looked so broken.

I don't remember what happened after that. I don't know how long I stayed there on that staircase. I don't remember my mom getting up off the floor. She did, though. She picked herself up and carried on.

Looking back on those events as an adult, I understand things so much better. As a child, I had no way of knowing what was happening. I had no way to manage the feelings I was having.

The next thing I recall was that a different man was in the house. I know there is a gap in the memories, but I don't know how long it was. It doesn't matter for this telling. What matters is that my dad was there, and things were normal, and then he wasn't, and they weren't normal anymore.

The different man in the house was fun. He played with us. Mom was happy again. Then she wasn't.

It turned out that this man was wearing a mask. He was fun on the surface, but he was an alcoholic and a thief. He stayed drunk. The fun didn't last long. My mother found out that he had been stealing what little money and valuables she had. She also found out that he was still married. Her marriage to him wasn't even valid. He even lied about that so that he could cozy up to her. He lived in our house and stole from her. After he was gone, she found the empty whisky bottles stashed all over the place.

One would think that my mother would learn from this great mistake. But who am I to judge? Maybe she did learn. She just didn't change herself. She was always looking for love, seeking out Mr. Right. She just happened to find the wrong kind of men.

Her break from my father broke her on a very fundamental level. Years later, she found a stable relationship with her third husband; well, technically her second husband since the lying, drunk thief didn't officially count.

As a teenager and young man, I was angry. I was confused. I blamed my mother and my father for many things. I still do, but now the blame is tempered with my own experience. I now know that, as fallible as they were, they were only doing what they could. My parents were dealing with life as it came at them. They were learning as they went.

As a kid, you think adults know everything, especially your parents. As an adult myself with children and grandchildren, I can tell you that we are all learning as we go. Sometimes we get it right. Most times, we do okay. Hopefully, we don't screw things up too badly.

I say this to let you know that I'm not telling you I have all the answers. I am still learning as I go. I have learned a lot along the way. It is these lessons, along with some excellent advice from those who actually do know what they are talking about, that I want to share with you. Lessons in improving your communication skills, advice on relationships, motivation to push yourself to take on new challenges, tips to get your budget under control and manage your debt, information on investing your hard-earned money, and more lessons along the way.

Please forgive me if I meander a little. It is okay. Life tends to take a meandering path.

Please forgive me if I get caught up in a tangent at times. I do so because I care. I will try to stay as much on topic as I can.

Forgive me if I make any errors. Please take what I say and do your own research. Look into these subjects more. Get educated on all of these topics. Please learn more than I know. I am not a professional in any of these fields. I am a person who has lived and learned.

Forgive me if I state what may at times be obvious to you. It may not be obvious to another reader.

With all that said, I want to thank you for taking the time to join me on this journey. Okay, here we go.

Chapter 1: Get Off the Wall

I grew up in a small town in Illinois. There were not many opportunities for upward mobility. I could work in a couple of different factories after graduating from high school. The pay wasn't bad, but unfortunately, this was the 80s, and there were a lot of layoffs happening.

When I entered high school, the unemployment rate was 10.2 percent, and inflation was as high as 14.76 percent. In November of 1981, the rate on a car loan was 17.36 percent. It eventually fell to 12.44 percent by May of 1989. Things were difficult, and choices were few.

I decided that I needed something different than what was right in front of me. I was no stranger to work. As I grew up, I took on a variety of jobs. I cut lawns and did general labor in the summer. In the winter, I shoveled snow around the neighborhood. I picked up jobs on local farms. I had a paper route. I worked as a pizza delivery person. I was a dishwasher.

I was a busboy. I also worked as a waiter. I needed something different. There were jobs available. The factory jobs paid okay, but as I said, they tended to get laid off regularly.

There had to be something else. Some other opportunity. That different thing came in the form of the Armed Services Vocational Battery (ASVAB) test, offered at my high school.

I clearly remember asking a friend of mine what it was when it was announced that it would be offered the next day. He told me it was a test to see if I could get into the military. I figured I would give it a shot. It might be better than working at factory A before being laid off, only to try to get in at factory B. I figured I had nothing to lose.

A few months later, a Navy Recruiter came to our school to meet with interested people. I was surprised when I was called into the guidance office to meet with him. I hadn't scheduled anything and hadn't even stopped at his table in the hall to talk with him. I found out that I had scored well in some of the sections he was interested in.

Fast forward a little, and I had made up my mind that out of the few choices I had, this was likely the best option. To be honest, I had seriously coasted in school. I did well enough on the tests, but I never applied myself to the homework. Really, why did I need to? I passed the classes. Oh, how very short-sighted I was.

Back to the fast-forward part. So, I had made up my mind to join the Navy. The only issue was that I was 17 and needed my mother's consent.

My mother and I did not have the best of relationships. By that time, I was living with my grandmother, and my mother lived a few hours away. I understand why my mother told me no. I really do. I even understood it then.

She was telling me no because she was afraid. She was afraid her child would join the military. She was afraid her child would be called upon to go into combat. It was the fall of 1985. Vietnam was still a very fresh memory. America withdrew from Vietnam on March 29, 1973. On November 4, 1979, a mob of 3,000 stormed the Tehran embassy, taking 63 American men and women hostage. They were held hostage for 444 days, finally being released on January 20, 1981. At the time, Iran and Iraq were at war (1980-1988).

Tensions over the line of death with Libya were very high, which would lead to conflict in March 1986. Tensions in the world were high, and here I was asking for her permission to join the military.

Yes, I understood she was scared. But, and this is a really big but, I knew what I wanted to do, and better yet, I knew why I wanted to do it.

I told her firmly that she could turn me down. She could refuse to sign the document and prevent me from joining the Navy…then. This was October. In March, I would turn 18.

I told her that if she chose to say no, I would go to the Navy recruiter on my 18th birthday and sign up then. The result would be the same. The only difference was whether she would try to hold me back or support me. It was a tense discussion. Ultimately, she chose to support me.

I joined the Navy Delayed Entry Program in October of my senior year. I remember how good it felt to know that I had a guaranteed job waiting for me after graduation. Not just a job but a possible career. The Navy was going to take me, a small-town kid, and train me and provide me a good paycheck. The pay was good for that time. Today, it doesn't seem like much money at all, but, then again, you have to think about having your home, utilities, food, uniforms, and all schooling paid for, plus that pay. It looked really good compared to working at factory A or B and being laid off whenever.

Navy: Never Again Volunteer Yourself

Before I left for basic training, my uncle shared some good advice. He said, "Keep your ears open, mouth shut, and always keep your head down." He was an Army Veteran. He served in the Vietnam War. He knew what he was talking about. He was speaking from his own experiences. That is key. I will keep coming back to this point as it is very important.

The first few hours of basic training for all branches of the military are chaotic and scary. Anyone who tells you different is lying to you, and they were probably lying to themselves to help them get through it.

After a while, you tend to recognize the patterns. Things move past the initial heart-pounding fear to a more throat-tight, sweaty-palms, racing-pulse type of situation. Still tense, but at a more manageable level.

Those people in charge, the ones wearing the crisp uniforms who had been yelling at everyone, were now asking my group if there were any volunteers. A guy next to me whispered, "Never Again Volunteer Yourself."

I had never heard that phrase before. I immediately thought of my uncle telling me to keep my head down. Good advice, right? But, like all advice, you have to be smart enough to know when to apply it.

The volunteers they were looking for would form a special company, while those who chose not to volunteer would proceed to the regular basic training company. I was curious, so I listened.

This special company would get the same training as everyone else, but it would be compressed. The company was a Drill Company. They were looking for people with band experience, preferably marching band. They also wanted people experienced in twirling flags or rifles.

I had no experience with any of that. They went on to say that we were being given this choice because our ASVAB scores were high enough to handle the compressed academic schedule. I had a choice to make. Keep my head down or volunteer. I chose to volunteer.

I have never regretted that decision. I enjoyed the challenge of learning how to be part of a team within a team. I was a member of the rifle drill team. We trained hard and became a precision unit.

I volunteered to take on more challenges and to challenge myself. I have never regretted my decision to join the Navy. It is, to this day, one of the best decisions of my life.

Take a Chance, Challenge Yourself

We are all presented with these decision points. Choose to do this, choose to do that, or choose to do nothing. No matter what, you are making choices. Through those choices, we navigate our lives. We can make the easy choice, or we can make the more challenging one. We can also choose not to make a choice and let our life proceed with our hands off the wheel and our foot off the gas pedal.

Go ahead, volunteer. Put yourself out there. What do you really have to lose? Sure, you may fail. You may also succeed. Things will change. That is life, though. Things *will* change. They will never stay the same. Put yourself out there. Whether you know it or not, you already are.

How can you improve if you are always holding yourself back? Crazy right? I said it, though. All too often, we are our own most significant obstacle. We don't allow ourselves to try. We kill our chances with self-doubt and self-defeating talk. *STOP IT!* You *CAN* do it. You should do it. You owe it to yourself to try.

How can you get to where you want to be if you don't take hold of your life? Grip that steering wheel tight and get to it, even if you don't have the foggiest idea where that is. Put yourself out there.

How do you set yourself out from the pack if all you do is hide among it? Stand up and be recognized. Take on the challenge.

Why you? Why not you? You know as much as the other person. If you don't know as much as they do, then study harder and learn more. You are as capable as the other person. Believe it! They are just as scared as you. They may hide it better, but they are worried about failing just like you are.

A popular saying I really like goes, "Hard work beats talent when talent doesn't work hard." This quote is attributed to Tim Notke, a high school basketball coach. The saying was made popular by NBA star Kevin Durant. It has been used in commercials and is frequently referenced. That is because it is true.

You cannot change what you came into the world with. You are going to be as tall as you are going to be. Your skin color, eye color, general body shape, and many other parts that make up your whole are immutable. You can work to refine your physical self through exercise. You can work on your intellect through study and the pursuit of education. You can work on how you view the world and the situations you face. You are in control of yourself.

It is up to you how much effort you put into defining and refining yourself. How much hard work are you willing to put in to separate yourself from others? More importantly, how much hard work are you willing to put in to find out how great you can be? You owe it to yourself to put in the work to become the best *you* that *you* can be.

Your peers fall across a spectrum. This is true in many ways, but for the sake of this discussion, let's focus on effort. You will naturally encounter some people who focus on doing the bare minimum to get by. The majority of people will do what is expected of them and not much more. They get through their day.

On the other end of the spectrum are those who do what is expected of them and look for ways to do it more efficiently. They look for ways to help others. They seek out opportunities that challenge them. They take on more difficult projects so they can learn. When they finish their expected workday, they invest their time in learning more and taking training that is not required. They put in the work. They set themselves apart from others.

What type of person have you been? Be honest with yourself. Remember, the only person you wake up with each morning and go to bed with each night of your life is you. Look at yourself in the mirror. Go ahead, I'll wait.

That is the person you must be honest with. It all starts right there. With you! Now, what type of person do you want to be? Get to it!

Back to my time in the Navy. You are expected to take on more responsibility. Part of that process is to advance up the rank structure.

Navy personnel are required to take a written exam for promotion to E4 through E7. These written tests cover general Navy knowledge and job- or rating-specific knowledge. I understand that all branches of the Armed Forces are similar in this regard.

The dates of these exams are published well in advance. People have time to study and prepare for them.

I can tell you from my own experience, as well as talking with my fellow sailors, that most people wait until the test date nears before they focus on studying.

Those of you who have not served in the military can relate as well. Remember back when you were in high school or college? How many times did you put off studying for a test or working on a project until the deadline was close?

The same applies here. Cramming for a test is never a good way to learn. We learn through repetition. The more repetition, the more we retain the lesson. When we cram for a test, we can retain some of the information, but only for a short time.

This also applies while you are attending a course. Taking time at the end of each day to review what was covered and going through a quick review of the material before class each day prepares you far more than just doing the minimum required.

Beginning your studies months before your promotion test date gives you time to thoroughly cover the material. It also gives you time to look more deeply into areas you may need to study more. Most importantly, it allows you the time to go over the key points repeatedly. Through repetition, you layer your knowledge. You build those connective pathways in your mind so they are strong and no longer temporary.

The people in the armed forces are a slice of everyday life. They fall across the same spectrums as the general public. I like to think they have more self-motivation in general, but by and large, the same principles apply. Most people are content to do just enough to get by. After work, they want a relaxing weekend.

I found that by setting aside a fixed amount of time each week to study for these tests, I was much better prepared and, as a result, had higher test scores. By putting in that extra effort, I was able to set myself apart from my peers.

It did not take much effort. It was discipline that made the difference. It wasn't just the tests that I did better on. I knew more about my job, which enabled me to become a better technician. I was disciplined and knowledgeable. I set myself apart by just doing a little more.

I applied that same discipline while pursuing my college degrees. I organized myself based on the assignments and their deadlines. I worked them daily. The amount of time I dedicated to each varied depending on other daily requirements, but I had a plan and stuck to it as much as I could. Little by little, day by day, assignment by assignment, I worked the plan. Course by course and degree by degree, I worked that plan.

At the start of a big, or sometimes not even that big, just new and intimidating task, it can feel overwhelming. I get it. I've been there many times. While I was a Navy recruiter, I met another highly successful recruiter. He and his team were crushing their assigned goals and winning many awards along the way. I asked him how he managed to juggle all of the tasks. It felt overwhelming.

He looked at me and asked me if I knew how to eat an elephant. What a crazy question to ask. It came out of nowhere, or so it seemed at first. He waited a minute for me to ponder the question before he continued. He simply said, "One bite at a time."

That was the pearl of wisdom he dropped on me. He watched me struggle to comprehend his meaning for a little bit before he elaborated. "Think about it," he said. "There is no way you can eat an elephant all at once. It is just too much to do.

On top of that, you can't do it all by yourself. You need help. There are others who can help you. In any case, the answer is simple," he said. "You do it one bite at a time."

This is not to say that I advocate eating elephants. I do not! They are great and majestic creatures and should be protected.

The lesson is plain when expressed in this exaggerated way. The task is simple when you break it down to the basic steps. It can be achieved by doing what needs to be done and keeping at it until you meet your goal. If you need help, get help. Remember, one bite at a time is how you get it done.

Discipline has served me very well throughout my adult life. I applied the same lessons in my professional career after the military. I have taken extra training to expand my knowledge beyond the basic requirements.

I have volunteered for additional assignments and team positions. It was not required. No judgment on those who want to attain the expected standard and do no more. You may not be reading this book anyway. Why would you? You are content with where you are in life. This book is for those who want to make more of themselves, who want to get somewhere other than where they are now. This book is for you.

I expected, and continue to expect, more from myself. Why? Because I know I can do it. I also know that it needs to be done in the end. If not me, then who? Who is going to step up? I'll volunteer for that. Never stop growing. Keep working to become the best you that you can be.

Let me share a situation with you. I had been on my first ship, a destroyer, for a few weeks. I was on duty, and part of that included sweeping the area of the ship my division was responsible for. It had rained the night before, so there were puddles to sweep overboard.

I completed my area and proceeded to sweep away the puddles in the next section. When the sailor responsible for that area saw me, he asked me what I was doing. I told him that it needed to be done. Yes, he said, but it isn't your responsibility. Why would you do that? My answer to him was simple. I reiterated that it needed to be done. He thanked me and kept sweeping away the water.

The point of this is to do that little bit extra. Help each other out. Don't just do the minimum when you can do more. Do more.

No one wants to fail, but failure is not bad in the long run. It is one event among many. You must be honest about it, though. Own up to it.

When reviewing what happened that led to that failure, you must be analytical. Do not make it personal at this junction. Do not focus on the fact that "you failed." Do not play the blame game. Don't justify it away. Own it. Assess it for what it is.

There are likely good points to take from it and move forward with. Go over the steps one by one. Assess what you were responsible for along the way. Look at what you could have done differently, if anything. If there was something you could have done differently, determine as much as you can what, if any, difference that alternate action may have had.

Really look at this scenario from as many different perspectives as possible. Break it down to the individual components. Learn from it. Evolve with those lessons. Give yourself room to grow.

When babies fall while learning to walk, they get up and try again. Football teams go to the locker room at halftime to assess how the first half of the game played out. Then they make adjustments and go out and try again.

It is okay to fall down. It is important to review what happened. Learn from it, get back up, and then do better. Keep going.

Do your best. Learn when you fall short. Learn when you succeed. More than likely, things did not go perfectly, even if it was a success. Learn from everything. Take the time to assess. Be honest and humble. Give credit to others. Recognize their efforts. Recognize yours as well.

A good method is to write down what happened at the end of each day. Make a conscious effort to capture your thoughts. We are all in a hurry to get to the next thing. There are constant demands on our time. Taking the time to review and reflect on what happened, then write it down, is a very valuable investment of your time. Believe it. Do it even when you are in a hurry. Make it a habit.

If you can do this at the end of significant events like meetings or interviews, or after a test, you will find it helpful as well. You have to be objective and honest. In a very short time, you will see the benefits of this process.

Get off the wall. What do you want to do that you have been avoiding?_____________________

What is holding you back?_________________

Commit to yourself! Take on the challenge. You got this.

<u>Chapter 2: Communication</u>

You need to read this chapter once to get a general understanding, and again to try to implement the lessons and minimize the everyday pitfalls I will discuss.

Communication is so important, yet we minimize its importance. We take it for granted. We all believe we are good communicators. That is not true. Stephen Covey said, "The biggest communication problem is we do not listen to understand. We listen to reply." You do not need to look far to see examples of that quote by Mr. Covey. It happens all too frequently. I know that I have fallen into that trap more often than I like. I make a conscious effort not to do so, but I still struggle with it at times.

I find that I do this more often when I am opposed to what the other person is saying. I must resist the temptation to prove that I am right and they are not. That is not communication. How can you communicate if you do not understand?

How can you understand if you are focused on what you are going to say and are not paying attention to what the other person is saying? That is not understanding. That is assuming. You are assuming you know what the other person is telling you. The big difference here is that you are assuming you already know and have stopped intentionally listening. Think about it for a minute. Really let it sink in.

It comes down to where your focus is. Are you focused on the conversation, or on saying what you want to say?

Have you ever known someone who jumps around while you are talking with them? Not physically jumping around. That would be weird. Do they leap to the end of their sentence, miss complete sentences, and jump to a conclusion without providing you a bridge to follow them?

If you know the person or the topic well, you can fill in some of the blanks and follow them. This is obviously not good communication.

Communication, at its simplest, is when a speaker sends a message, either verbal or written, to a receiver. That's it, really. So very simple. And yet, we struggle with good communication.

There is a difference between communication and good communication. A person can be doing their best to communicate their message and still fail. Remember, communication is based on at least two people. If the receiver is not receptive to the message, then communication fails; the messenger's intention fails.

In this case, the message may result in a negative response, an unintended response, or an action. More on that later. If the message is in a language the receiver does not understand, there can be no communication, even though the sender is doing their best to convey it. That foreign language can also be technical, and the receiver may not fully understand it. The message must be targeted at the receiver. It needs to be at the level of complexity appropriate for them.

Picture this with me, if you will. A young boy stands on a soapbox, yelling out: "Get your paper. Get your paper here! Farmer MacDonald's cow broke the fence again."

People are walking past him and not paying any attention. They are in the city. What do they care about a cow breaking down a fence? Now, if that cow was blocking traffic, that could change their interest and make the message meaningful to them. If that cow turned onto the sidewalk and ran at them, it would become very meaningful.

If the message isn't relevant to the receiver, they likely won't be interested. If they are not interested, there is little chance they will invest their time in learning more about it.

So, with all of that out of the way, how can you communicate better? What actions can you take? Here are ten things you can do right now.

1. Listen: This is not a passive action. Really listen to the message being communicated to you. Listen to understand what they are trying to communicate. Do not make assumptions. Listen! Listen to the context. Listen to the *way* they communicate the message to you. Not just the words. Listen to their delivery and how they focus on certain points over others. Really listen to them. Listen to understand.

2. Ask questions: A lot of communication breaks down at this point. Many times, people, myself included, ask questions to support their position and try to win. Do not do this! This is a quick way to break down any hope of communication. It will lead to an argument and not a discussion.

   Instead, ask clarifying questions to better understand the message. Something like "Just so I am clear, are you saying water is blue?" Or, "Can you tell us more about why you believe people should listen more?" How can you begin to say anything if you do not understand what you are talking about? How can you really understand if you don't try?

3. Communicate clearly: The first step is to understand what you want to communicate. What is your message? Why do you want to say this? What is your intention? In this instance, you are replying to the communication that originated from someone else. Respond to this. Do not switch it to something else to support your position. This is communication. Stay focused on the discussion.

4. Listen: It is time to see how others respond to what you have said. How receptive are they to it? Did they understand what you intended to communicate? Are they staying focused on the direction of the conversation, or are they jumping around?

5. Stay focused: Do not make it personal. Make it about the discussion. Make it about the facts. Support the facts when they are facts. Know and accept the difference between facts and

opinions. If you heard something and believe it, say it like that. Say you *believe* it to be true.

Do not take a belief and present it as a fact. Everyone is entitled to their beliefs. We must accept that. We do not have to believe in the same things. We must listen to others and respect their beliefs. We must also be resolute in our beliefs. We do not discredit someone based on their beliefs. We do not allow others to do it to us either. Respect is the key. Respect their positions and expect respect for yours.

6. Be receptive: Listen. Yes, I know I am being repetitive, but so is this skill. Listening is critical. You must resist the urge to shut down just because you disagree with what someone is telling you. They just might be right. Oh, perish the thought. Even if everything they say isn't correct, there may be points that are. There may be lessons you can learn just by learning how someone might be looking at things differently from you. Be open to their ideas and points of view. How can we ever grow if we do not entertain new ideas or points of view?

7. Be engaged: A conversation can, and typically does, flow between the participants. The person who is making a point of discussion needs to have the freedom to present their points fully. The others involved are responsible for asking clarifying questions to understand the points being made. This process may take a winding path. Be engaged and maintain your focus. It is tempting to follow a point or counterpoint, but be careful not to veer from the main point. Bring it back when it is veering astray. This also applies to your internal thought processes—reign in the urge to follow thoughts that go astray. Stay engaged in the conversation flow. Make your mental notes to add to the conversation, but don't let them distract you from the conversation itself.

8. Be prepared: When entering a discussion, any discussion, you will be more successful if you know what you are getting into. Be knowledgeable of the setting, context, those involved, and, of course, the topic of conversation itself. While you may not be able to be fully prepared for all or any of these things, you will further your capacity for engagement and ultimately your

understanding by being as prepared as possible.

We are all faced with situations that may involve challenging conversations. Family events, like holiday get-togethers, can bring out different personalities and views on situations. Conversations about family members or friends who were involved in situations can lead to discussions about what they should or should not have done or known. Discussions on local, national, or international events can elicit strong opinions. Knowledge of those involved can prepare you better for those conversations. Focusing on the topics themselves, rather than proving that you are right and they are wrong, can actually lead to good discussions. You can disagree with someone and still have a very good conversation as long as it is non-judgmental and open to differing viewpoints.

Knowledge of where someone is coming from is important. We all view things from our own perspective. It takes effort to get out of our own heads and viewpoints to look at things from others' perspectives. I am not saying the old trope of: If I were you, I would... That rarely goes well. You are *not* them. You cannot fix their problems for them. You cannot make them see things as you do unless you communicate with them. Communicate with them patiently, thoroughly, and openly. Help them to see where you are coming from to face the discussion.

9. Be empathetic: We each have walked our own path getting to where we are. We are all different. We do not all have the same beliefs. We do not all agree on how to pronounce *tomato*. We must be empathetic to where others are. We must be open to them. We must take ourselves out of ourselves and listen and try to understand, as much as is possible, to that other person.

10. You do not know everything: That is okay. You do not have to prove you are the most intelligent person in the room or even in the conversation. If you try to prove you are the smartest, you will likely prove that you are not. Possessing the knowledge and self-awareness to know that you can always learn from another person truly makes you interesting. You will naturally be more engaging and interesting. A conversation is a sharing of

information. No one knows everything about everything, and that is okay. Be open to admitting that. Admit it to yourself. Never be afraid to admit it to others, either. Be willing to acknowledge others' knowledge. We can and should learn something from every person and situation we encounter. Never stop learning.

There is something else I want to say here. You are in control of your communication. It is up to you to ensure you are working to be a better communicator. You are not responsible for someone who is not exercising these traits.

Another tactic I encourage you to use is to separate your emotional self from the conversation. We can never thoroughly tamp down our emotions, nor would we want to. We also do not want them to take control of us. Our emotions can cloud our thinking very quickly. They can make us focus too much on some things and discard others. We all have certain things that can trigger us, things that can instantly make us focused and defensive. We can quickly go from communicating to arguing. Just as bad, we can center the conversation only on those things we emotionally focus on and believe it went a way that, in reality, it did not.

Keep your emotions in check. Focus on what is being said. Focus on the person who is saying it. Why may they be saying it? Where are they coming from? Seek to understand not only what they are saying, but also why. Try to understand the why of what they are saying, not your preconceived ideas. While you are seeking to understand, keep your feelings in check. This part is not about you. It is about them.

They are communicating. It is your job to receive that communication from that sender. Seek to understand them. I am not saying you have to agree with them. This is a conversation. There are likely many points of similarity if you are open to listening for them. Even when things are not what you agree with, you may, and probably will, learn more about the position the other person is coming from. Be open. Be empathetic. Be receptive. Be respectful.

When it is your turn to communicate, stay on topic. Do not change the focus abruptly just to make your point. That is not a discussion. Talk about the issue in the conversation.

Did you pick up on how many "yous" are in the previous two paragraphs? The reason is as evident as the repetitive use of the word you. You are in control.

If you find yourself in a setting where someone is not listening to you, not seeking to understand you, and not being empathetic, know that you are likely not in a conversation. Conversations go back and forth.

If it is not a situation you can extract yourself from, know that the communication is directive in nature. This is necessary in the work setting, in the classroom, and in some family settings. If it is not this type of setting, it may be appropriate to disengage.

You cannot make someone see things as you do. Their perspective is their choice, as it is yours. Some people are very content with how they perceive the world around them and absolutely do not want to change. If that is the case, your efforts will, at best, be fruitless, and, at worst, escalate into arguments. Be empathetic and aware enough to know when it is appropriate to move on.

Never be afraid to say you were wrong about something. This does not mean you're showing weakness. Rather, it shows your capacity for growth and humility, and that you are open to learning.

People mistake admitting errors as a sign of weakness. You likely associate with people who are similar to you. They likely have knowledge in similar areas. Surprise, surprise, they likely know enough to figure out when you are wrong and when you are right.

If you are the type of person who does not admit your mistakes, you can be seen as arrogant and insecure in your knowledge or position in the world. If you are questioned, others may see your weaknesses. Let it go. Don't be so concerned about what others think. You can't control someone else's thoughts. Owning your mistakes is not a weakness. It is being human. We all make mistakes. It is how you recover from them that shows your strength.

Being open to learning means being open to making mistakes. Learn from your own mistakes as well as others'. Stay focused on growing. Acknowledge others' efforts, and they will acknowledge yours.

Okay, now that we have gone through the basics of communication, it is time to look at how to use these tools in the real world. How much more real can we get than when discussing relationships?

Relationships are many and varied. They evolve and devolve over time, and hopefully evolve yet again. Relationships are based upon communication when we get right down to it. Communication is how we get to know each other. It is how we discuss our wants and our needs. Relationships are built upon the evolution of our interactions. We learn to trust each other. We learn who to reach out to for our varied needs. We also learn who to avoid in various situations.

Let's begin with our immediate circle, the ones we are closest to—those we live with or closely associate with, including our family, partners, friends, and roommates. One of the significant components of communication is engagement. Managing engagement has always been a challenge.

We constantly struggle to manage our engagement amidst the multitude of distractions we encounter. We have homework to do, projects to work on, laundry to wash, and groceries that won't just appear in the refrigerator.

We also have deadlines at the office, customers to satisfy, and travel time between school, work, and shopping. Then we have friends and family to keep up with, and finally, after all that, we have to communicate with those closest to us.

It is clear just how important it is to communicate clearly. And yet, we often don't. We don't take the time to tell those closest to us how important they are to us. We don't take the time to ask them how they are really doing. We don't make a conscious effort to engage with them.

Be present in their space and time. Be focused on them, where they are, and what they are dealing with.

Listen. Yes, we are back to listening again. Listen intentionally to them. Demonstrate active empathy for where they are and what they are going through. Not based on your feelings or opinions. Not judging whether they are being too much or not enough of anything. Postpone judgment! Be there! It is so simple and never easy.

Push away the noise and focus on them. Don't let the ding of a message distract you. Don't pick up the call unless you know there is a situation that really, and I mean really, needs your immediate attention. Be present. Be focused. Be engaged. Be empathetic. Be clear with your communication. It truly matters.

Don't assume someone knows what you're thinking or feeling. They probably have a good idea, but that is not the same as them knowing.

If it matters to you, communicate it.

Communicate what is on your mind.

Communicate what is in your heart.

This is not to be confused with blame. Blaming someone else is rarely a path to a good solution. Hold yourself accountable and speak to what you feel, think, know, and believe. When it is appropriate to hold someone else accountable, do so by clearly communicating what has been done.

Do not speak to what you believe to be someone else's intentions. That is up to them to communicate. Don't shout out, "You never even meant to come to my parents' for dinner." You assume it's true, but it may not be.

Do not assume. Let them speak for themselves. Ask the specific question. "Did you ever intend to come to my parents' for dinner tonight?"

Now listen. Let them speak. Hear what they say. Then, when you fully understand what they said, clearly communicate what you think of their explanation.

When someone speaks with you, you know they are telling you things from their point of view. They are communicating based on their perspective on things as they perceived them throughout their life up to that point.

Be patient and perceptive to that. Seek understanding as much as possible and when appropriate. Sometimes, the best thing you can do is just be quiet and listen. Let the other person talk it through. You do not need to fix it right then and there. Be present. Be engaged.

Your lack of engagement can speak as loudly as your engagement. Be cautious about how you invest your time. I assure you that the time you spend engaged with the people you care about is going to matter much more than the time you spend looking at cute cat videos or swiping through interesting pictures. Be present. Be engaged. It matters. It communicates so much.

One area of the communication process I recognize I struggle with:_______________________

One area I am committed to:

____

What area of communication do you want to learn more about?_______________________

Chapter 3: Emotional Intelligence

If the title of this chapter gives you a negative feeling, I encourage you to suspend that thought. This is not a feel-good, sappy topic. Using emotional intelligence is hard. It is not for the faint of heart. If you are strong enough to do this, you will benefit.

I am going to cover emotional intelligence at a very high level. I encourage you to learn more about this topic on your own. You will benefit from knowing more about emotional intelligence, or EI for short. I will also go into personality indexing, again from a high overview. I will be discussing both topics in the same chapter because they complement each other so well.

We all have emotions, and those emotions play a large part in our personalities. The more we know about these things, the better we are able to understand ourselves. Knowing this, we can better understand why we react to specific events or triggers. We can learn to manage those feelings better and control our behaviors in certain situations, well, really in all situations.

We can then take this knowledge and look outward with it. We can better understand why others react as they do. We can utilize this knowledge to communicate more effectively with others. We can better anticipate how others will respond in specific situations.

With practice and further study, you will be able to identify events that are likely to elicit specific reactions from individuals. By understanding their personality, you can anticipate different reactions from individuals with specific personality traits. You likely will begin to see them when you finish this chapter.

Emotional intelligence is the capacity to recognize, understand, manage, and utilize emotions effectively in oneself and others.

Let's apply this definition of emotional intelligence to what we discussed in Chapter 2, where we looked at communication in its basic form. We then learned that communicating quickly becomes complicated. To complicate it further, let's remember that we are talking about people. People are complicated. We are made up of many things that have come together at one moment to make us who we are.

Our personalities are a combination of nature and nurture. We are born with certain characteristics that we demonstrate in our actions and reactions. We then learn from our experiences—inputs from family, environment, community, as well as many other external factors. All these components come together to form a self. It is all very complex.

Personality indexing categorizes how you respond to situations.

- Are you the type of person who likes to take charge of the situation?
- Do you believe your ideas are the best? Do you thrive on stress and seek wins?
- Do you tend to make quick decisions and get frustrated when others do not?
- Or are you the type of person who needs more information, more details? Do you prefer to analyze the situation and methodically review the information before making a decision?
- Do you get upset when others try to rush you to make a decision? Do you look at others as being too quick to rush to a decision without considering all the facts?
- Are you the type of person who prefers to reach a consensus within the group? Do you consider what is best for the majority before making your decision? Do you prefer the role of facilitator to that of leader? Do

> you try to involve as many people as
> possible?
> - Are you the type of person who likes details
> but does not prefer going into the weeds?

Some people fit exactly into these categorizations and rarely deviate from them. There is another group that doesn't stay in these roles. They float between them based on the situation.

In fact, we all do that to some degree. Imagine this scenario, if you would. If you are driving your car and get a flat tire, you do not discuss it with the other people in the car to determine what action to take, although some of your passengers may volunteer their input. The situation does not give you the time to reach a consensus. Each second counts. You make the best decision you can based on the information you have. You control the vehicle, pull over to the side of the road when and where it is safe to do so, let out the breath you have been unconsciously holding, release the death grip you have on the steering wheel, check on your passengers to ensure they are all good, and deal with the flat tire safely and quickly.

The situation you are in will shape how you process information. It will dictate the parameters for gathering and interpreting that information. Each situation is different and will require different responses. Ideally, you have enough time to gather information and then make the best decision possible.

There is no one better type of personality. Each category has advantages and potential hazards. You must learn to recognize your personality and how you prefer to approach and manage situations. Once you have done this, you need to apply it to those people you deal with.

Knowing that someone is the type of person who likes to take charge and likes their ideas, but doesn't necessarily like to take the time to conduct thorough research or even go into detailed discussions, will help you to interact better with them. If you are the type of person who likes to take charge, knowing that others are not like you and accepting that it is okay if they are not, will help you work with and collaborate with them.

Very detail-oriented people may frustrate the take-charge, make-quick-decisions personality type, as they like to take more time to assess things. In contrast, people who typically take charge prefer to assess the situation quickly and act decisively. Analytical personality types will get frustrated with those types and often attribute their decisiveness to not analyzing the facts thoroughly enough to make the best decisions.

I am sure you can quickly see how these two types of individuals can irritate each other. The truth of the matter is that there is no set right way to do things. These are the ways that people manage situations based on their personality types. Each type has advantages and disadvantages. The situation also must be taken into account.

Remember that each situation is unique unto itself. A decision may need to be made quickly. There may not be time to analyze the details in any depth. If an out-of-control car is coming at you, there is no time to assess the situation in great detail. You need to do everything you can to get yourself and, hopefully, any other people out of the way. It is only when you are safe that further analysis is warranted.

Another situation may warrant a very detailed analysis, and rushing it will only cause problems. The situation may be better served by group consensus rather than relying on a single person to direct the outcome.

Understanding personality types will help you to better understand and interact with people. You will also be better able to appreciate the best people to perform in different situations.

What personality type are you?________________

<u>Chapter 4: Relationships</u>

You are in control of *you*. You are not in control of another person. You cannot make them feel something different than what they feel.

You are in control of *you*. You cannot make someone change. If another person wants to change, they will do so because they want to. If they change because you want it, they will likely not continue with that change. They are in control of themselves, and *you* are in control of *you*.

We are, each and every one of us, on our own path through life. Each of us is unique. We perceive our world through our own senses. A person who is color blind sees things differently from others. Some people perceive sounds as colors, a condition known as synesthesia. Some people have the ability to differentiate many more shades of color than others can. These differences are completely normal for each person, as to how they are.

We have our own experiences that we perceive from our vantage points. We evaluate those experiences based on the sum of everything we have experienced up to that moment. We share experiences with others in that moment. We share our interactions with family and friends. We relate our experiences to those who are close to us.

Each person we choose to allow close to us is a deliberate choice. Our family is our family. The people we go to school with and those we work with are, by and large, not our choice. That is not to say that you cannot or should not be close to your family members. Some of you—hopefully most of you—have good relationships with at least some family members. Treasure them! Those people have known you longer than everyone else.

Our time is limited. There are only 1,440 minutes in each day. We usually spend eight to nine hours a day at school or work during the week. We each sleep about eight hours a night. We need to get ready and get to where we are going, so let's say that takes two hours each day. Suffice it to say, we have limited time left for what we decide to do and with whom we decide to spend that time with.

When we find someone we actually want to spend our time with, and they want to be with us too, it is something really special. We need to treat this special connection as truly special as it is. Out of all of the people you know, that person is the one you are choosing to spend your personal time with. That person is also choosing to be with you. Despite all of the faults you know about yourself, they want to be with YOU. That is special. They are special. Make sure they know how special they are to you. Love is intentional. Every day, make it your intention to let that person know how special they are to you.

Why, then, do we fade into complacency? Why do we take the person who really matters to us for granted? Why do we settle into ourselves? Because it takes effort. We have to work at it. We have to stay invested.

If you are going to be in, then be all in!

Give of yourself without expecting anything in return. Give because you love. Give because it is the right thing to do. Give of yourself.

Do not lose sight of yourself. If you give freely and do so because you want your partner to enjoy what you are giving, whether that is a single flower, treating them out to dinner just because, picking up a unique rock because you were thinking of them, or whatever is appropriate for that person and your relationship, then it is good and right. If you are doing it to make them happy so they will act better, whatever that may mean to you, then it is wrong. That is manipulative behavior. You need to do it just for their benefit.

When you give freely with no expectations, you will realize that the returns far outweigh the effort you may make.

This, of course, is based upon the assumption that you are in a healthy relationship. If you are the giver and your partner is a taker by nature, you will likely need to reassess the relationship.

If you are in a relationship with someone who is acting jealously, there is a reason for it. The reason is because of one or both of you. Is the reason due to something that is, or is perceived to be, happening now? Is the reason because of something that happened in the past?

If you are giving your partner reasons to be jealous, you have some decisions to make. Are you willing to stop those behaviors? If so, do not do it for your partner. Do it for you.

This may sound strange if you are stepping out of your relationship. Why would you stop if you are doing it for you? If you want a meaningful relationship with your partner, there must be trust.

I have to put in a disclaimer here for those who have an open relationship. If that is you, then I am confident that you have established your boundaries. In your relationship, you understand what works for both of you. There is trust in that. Do what works for you. Do what works for both of you.

For those who are not in an open relationship but are stepping out the door anyway, I will continue.

If you know you are causing your partner pain, you need to be honest, even if you haven't been caught yet. If it will cause them pain when they find out. Be honest with yourself first and foremost.

Are you willing to stop cheating on your partner? If not, then you need to let your partner go. If you are cheating on them, then they are not your partner. You are acting solo.

Sure, they are your partner in most things. But most is not all. If it is not all, then are they really your partner? Be all in.

If you do want to be in a meaningful relationship, not just meaningful to you but to your partner as well, then you must stop and be invested in your relationship. Do it for yourself. You owe it to yourself, and you most definitely owe it to your partner, assuming, of course, that they are committed to your relationship too. Remember that there are two people involved, and each one needs to do the right thing for themselves.

If you are in a relationship with someone who is cheating on you, then you must be honest with yourself. You have to admit that it is really happening. Don't tell yourself it isn't going on if you really know it is. You owe it to yourself more than that. Seriously, take a look in the mirror and be honest with yourself.

You deserve to be in a relationship with a committed and trustworthy partner. If the person is not committed to you, then you need to acknowledge that. You need to have an honest conversation with them. I am not saying to fight. Have a conversation. Clearly talk about what you believe or know is happening. Talk about how you feel about it. DO NOT SAY what they think or how they feel. Only talk about yourself.

After this difficult discussion, you have some decisions to make. Do you believe what you are being told? If compromises are made, do you feel comfortable with them? Do not think for a minute that you can change the other person. You can't do it. You are responsible for yourself. They are responsible for themselves.

You also must know that people usually do not change. They may try. They may really want to change, in that moment, but they are who they are, and they do what they do for their reasons.

This is not to say they cannot change; just that most people, in most cases, revert to their previous behavior. Know that it is a long shot. Be honest with yourself.

You deserve to be in a relationship where you are equals, partners. A relationship that gives you as much as you give back. It needs to be balanced over time. Relationships that have a giver and a taker cannot be good in the long run unless those roles flow from one to the other. The giver ends up spent, and the taker is never satisfied. There is no partnership. You owe it to yourself to have better.

If you are in a relationship where there is jealousy but neither partner is stepping out, there may be other reasons for it. We all bring to relationships everything we have learned and experienced up to that point.

We bring both the good and the not-so-good. If we were in a relationship where we were cheated on and lied to, we know that those lessons were hard learned, and there likely are defenses and triggers in place that have nothing to do with you. You are just getting to know each other.

As humans, we are experiential learners. Our hands get burned when we put them over the fire. We learn not to get it so close to the fire again.

When we are cheated on and lied to until we find out and call an end to the relationship, we learn from the pain and deceit. We learn to look for the signs we should have acknowledged in that past relationship. We also probably learn not to trust as freely.

I have been in this situation. My first wife was unfaithful, multiple times with multiple partners. I was young. I wanted to make it work so badly, not because of my love for her. I wanted to make it work because my parents' marriage didn't work. I thought that if I just loved her enough, if I was understanding enough, gave her enough, she would stop cheating and be my good wife.

Believe me when I tell you that you cannot make someone change. It is entirely up to that person, and that change probably will not last even if they try. They are who they are, and they do what they do because of everything they are and everything they have done and experienced before they ever even met you.

Over time, I became honest with myself and took responsibility for my choices. I learned many lessons going through this very difficult time. I learned about myself. I opened my eyes. I moved on and kept doing the best I could. I kept those painful lessons close to my heart.

Years later, while I was dating the woman who would, in time, become my second wife, she asked me why I didn't get jealous. I knew the answer to this question. It was a decision I made based on lessons from my first marriage.

I told her that there was no reason for me to be jealous. If she wasn't doing anything for me to be jealous of, why should I be jealous? If, however, she was doing things that I should be jealous of, then we were over. I would not put up with that in a relationship. I told her that if I couldn't trust her, we could not be in a relationship. There simply was no reason for me to be jealous.

We can learn to trust again. It takes time, patience, and, above all, honesty. Honesty and trust are the true foundations of any good relationship.

It is important to be honest about why you are feeling jealous. It is crucial to respond with openness. Address the jealous feelings. Do not discount them. The feelings are real, even if they are unfounded in your current relationship.

If you find that you are being jealous because of something that has happened to you in a past relationship, you must acknowledge that to yourself. Remember, you have to be honest with yourself before all else. If your partner is not giving you reasons to be jealous, you should be honest with them, too. We are individuals. Because your previous partner cheated and hurt you, that does not mean that your current one will.

I am not saying to put blinders on. The saying "once burned and twice shy" is not a bad way to go. Learn from your life lessons, but do not judge harshly unless it is deserved. We all have baggage. There is no way we could have gotten this far in our journey without our baggage.

That doesn't mean you have to unpack it all the time and let it clutter up your current life. It is okay to take parts of it out from time to time and examine them individually. It surely doesn't mean you should unpack it all at once as soon as you arrive in a relationship and announce: "Here I am! Deal with it!"

You will likely find that they deal with it by wishing you well as you find your way on your journey without them.

Behaviors, both real and perceived, can cause problems. Hanging out with friends can cause jealousy. This can go both ways. If spending too much time with friends is getting in the way of the limited time you have for your partner, that is a problem.

On the other hand, when you got into your relationship, you likely found out or already knew your partner had a strong relationship with their friend or friends. Here, we go back to communication. This needs to be talked about. Open and honest communication is crucial.

Making your partner limit their time with friends so that you can demonstrate your control is horrible behavior. If you are the type who must be in control, exercise that control over yourself. Acknowledge this side of you and do something about it. We are responsible for ourselves and our actions, just as we are responsible for controlling ourselves. We are not responsible, nor do we have the ability, to control others.

Do not be insensitive to your partner. Don't expect them to always entertain your friends. Don't sacrifice your couple time just to hang out with your friends all the time. This is terrible, too.

Talk about it. Talk about what is important to you. Talk about what you will and will not feel good about. If you are not willing to cut back on your time with your friends, that is your decision. You are in a relationship with your friends, too. Your partner should seek a relationship with someone who will be as invested in them as you are with your friends. You are being true to you. They need to be true to themself.

Communication in a relationship is vital. Without it, there is no way you will really know one another. You may think you do, but what you really end up learning is each other's expectations and impressions. You know what the other person showed you and chose to share. If they are not sharing with you, then they are already leaving the relationship. They are shutting down. They have made up their mind that the effort is no longer worth it.

Good relationships are built on healthy and open communication. It is not easy. Being open to listening to your partner takes effort. To listen, you have to be engaged. You have to make the effort. This is not passive hearing, as you are busy watching television or playing video games. If you are scrolling through your phone, then your focus is not fully on the conversation. On the other hand, you should choose when to have difficult conversations. Do not expect your partner to be fully engaged if you talk with them during your favorite binge-watching session on your streaming service.

If it is an important conversation, make sure that you give it the attention it deserves. Minimize distractions so you can both focus. Be open. Be honest. Be receptive. Be respectful. Be considerate. Be present.

Do not keep bringing up past issues. They may be relevant or not. The point is that, whatever happened, you probably addressed it at that time. You probably had a discussion or a fight about it and then decided to forgive them and move on.

If you keep bringing it up, you have not moved on or forgiven your partner. That is not fair to them or to you. If you really can't forgive them and move on, then it is a much bigger problem than you are acknowledging, and you need to either get help for it, or maybe it is time to move on from each other.

If, however, it really is not that big an issue and you are using it to bolster your current position or argument, or to cause them pain, then you must STOP! That behavior is destructive and has no place in a healthy relationship.

If you are hiding purchases from each other, that is a problem. Why are you hiding them? Are you worried your partner will get upset if they find out? Is it about the things you are buying? Are you spending money on things you have agreed you wouldn't anymore?

If this is the case, you need to really think about why you are still choosing to do it. You said you wouldn't, so why are you? If you really have no intention of stopping, you need to be honest about that. It will be a difficult conversation for sure.

Don't be the person who goes out and spends the rent money, then makes up lies about where it went. Be honest with each other. Be honest with yourself.

If you are the one who is constantly being responsible and paying the bills while your partner comes up with excuses, yet again, about how they don't have enough money to pay their way, then it is time to look in the mirror. Go ahead, I'll wait.

Now look at the most important person in your world. You owe it to that person to have a partner who is a partner. It is going to be a difficult conversation, but it is okay to expect better. It is okay to demand better. It is okay to end it and be better.

It is widely acknowledged that finances can cause significant issues in relationships. Sure, while the expenditure of money can cause grief, I assert that the central problem is communication or, in this case, a lack of communication.

Open communication is critical in a good relationship. I told you about what I told my second wife about my lack of jealousy. I wish I had been as assertive with her about other boundaries, lines I would not cross. That lack of communication, along with subsequent actions, caused many problems.

I was in Sicily with my two little children from my first marriage when I met my second wife. Being a single parent is hard. It is especially hard to be a single parent in the military, living in a foreign country. When we start a new relationship, we show our new partner our best selves. We pick up the empty plates off the coffee table before they come over. What we usually don't do is have difficult conversations. We assume the other person knows how we feel. They know how we think. They know what we want.

You are committing to spend time with that other person. Why not make your expectations clear? I really wish I had.

She was polite. She was kind. She was fun. We got along very well. She knew I was in the Navy. She knew my kids and got along well with them. She told me that when she was in high school, she really wanted to travel to America.

It all sounded good. I wanted to be in a good relationship. I wanted a good person to serve as a mother to my children. Their biological mother did not contest my having custody of them and was not in contact with them.

I should have had some difficult but reasonable conversations with her before asking her to marry me. Instead of assuming she wanted to be a mother to my children, we should have talked about it in detail. We should have discussed our expectations. We should have discussed what married life in the Navy is like.

We should have talked about leaving her home in Sicily and going where the Navy sent us. We should have talked about what it meant for her when we got to that foreign country, and I had to deploy, leaving for extended periods. Those were serious subjects we should have talked about ahead of time. I really wish we had. Maybe things would have been different.

I came to learn that she did not want to be the mother to my children. She didn't want to raise someone else's kids. By this time, we had our first child together.

Yes, I saw signs along the way. There were issues. I thought that she would get used to the way I wanted things to be. Meanwhile, she was thinking I would change my points of view. We should have talked about those big issues. If we had talked about them, we would not have reached the critical point we did.

I knew it wasn't healthy for my children to be exposed to the fights we were having, especially my older two. They didn't need to hear the way she spoke to me. They did not need to see the way I avoided her. It was an unhealthy environment for everyone involved.

I made the toughest decision of my life to that point. I decided to ask my mother to care for my first two children. She agreed to give them a stable home. I knew it was best for them to get away from the chaos that had become my life.

In time, things calmed down. Life moved on. My first two children were safe in America. My third child was growing up, and we were expecting our fourth. Things had calmed down, but they were not good between us. Life went on. The kids grew up. Our relationship became colder. She wasn't happy. I wasn't happy. We weren't talking about anything with substance. We were cohabitating.

She wasn't happy being away from her country. I wasn't happy she was with me. The problem was that I loved being with my children, at least the two that were still with me. Every time I reached out to my other kids, it led to a fight. She had control issues.

She did not have control, and she had an issue with that. Nobody has total control of life. We all have to try to make the best decisions we can and learn from our mistakes. She struggled with depression as well as some other issues.

She increasingly said that the lack of sunshine in Germany made her depression worse. This is a real thing that affects people. I can't say whether this was true for her. I can tell you that she was not happy. She was bitter. The relationship between us was bad.

A home where parents avoid each other is not a place where children can thrive. It shows them too many examples of how things should not be.

This lasted until my youngest finished kindergarten. Every year, they would go on vacation in Italy for the summer. I was very surprised she decided to return in August. I really thought she would stay in Italy and tell me it was over.

I was close to being correct. She came back to tell me in person that it was over. Well, she told me she needed a break and asked if I would give her a year to make up her mind. I told her I would. I knew it had been over for years, and I knew that a year or any amount of time would not change that. It was time to end it.

I drove them from where we were stationed in Germany to her hometown in Sicily. That trip to drop them off was excruciating. Knowing that I would leave my kids there. Knowing they wouldn't be with me anymore hurt deeply. I was losing my kids a second time. It hurt just as bad.

That drive back to Germany, all alone in the car, was soul-crushing. The drive was a blur. Another stab in the heart came the first morning, waking up to a silent house. Coming home from work to that silent house day after day, week after week, hurt every single time. One of the things I had absolutely loved was opening my front door, having my kids run to me, and wrapping me in a big hug. They were not there anymore. I opened the door, stood there, and nothing. That deafening silence still echoes in my heart.

That year, I had told her I would give her passed without either of us ever telling the other that we missed each other. I didn't miss her. As I said, it had been over for a long time.

I did miss my children, and I told them every single day. I still make a conscious effort to talk with all of my children as often as I can and tell them I miss them.

I wish I had had those difficult conversations at the beginning of our relationship. Would it have made a difference? Yes, I am sure it would have. What would my life look like if I had? I have no way of knowing. I wish I had communicated what I wanted and what I expected from the relationship.

Please try to do better than I did. I hope it will bring you fewer challenges and much less pain and heartache.

Being honest and upfront about your intentions, actions, plans, and goals is always the best path. It is better than hiding things from each other. It is better than lying to each other. Have that difficult talk. Put it out there and then make decisions based on that talk.

You cannot change another person. You can set the example. You can make suggestions and recommendations. You can provide information on where they can get help, counseling, or other support. You cannot fix them. Each of us has to fix ourselves. It is the only way.

It has taken me a long time. There have been many mistakes along the way. I have learned a lot. I have matured a lot. Due to a very interesting confluence of circumstances, I met the love of my life. Of course, at the time I didn't know it.

I knew she was smart, focused, determined, caring, and funny. I knew she was beautiful. Even more so, she had a beautiful soul. We had a great deal of things in common. We liked a lot of the same things. We had been through similar life experiences. We liked being together. We still do. She is my best friend.

We've been together for ten years now. I am grateful she chose me to spend her life with. She motivates me to be better, to do better. She is the person I seek advice from, the one I bounce my ideas off of. She is the face I see before I go to sleep at night and the face I wake to each morning. I have found my partner.

This is not to say that we don't have our disagreements. Many come readily to mind. "Put that rock over there," she says while my back is to her. I set the rock down and immediately hear her correct me. "Not there. Put it more to the left." I do so. "No, no, put it to the left." I let out a long breath. Stand up and stretch my back. Did I mention this is a rather large rock?

I turn to her and see that she is frustrated that I am not understanding her. I know she has a much better eye for these types of things than I do. We are constructing a pond in our backyard, and these rocks are both functional and decorative. From where she is standing, she has a much better perspective on how the rock looks in relation to the others around it.

I am frustrated that I don't understand how I am not following her simple directions. I am sure she is feeling the same. Instead of picking up the heavy rock again and moving it even more, I resolve to keep it simple. "Should it be here or here?" I ask, pointing to the two places I see as possibilities.

"Yes, that one," is her reply.

I smile a little and point to the last place I indicated. "So here?"

"Yes, there," she agrees.

I put the rock in place, stand, and step to the side so she can clearly see it and how it fits with the other rocks.

"Could you turn it?" she asks.

Remember our discussion about communication, where the receiver is to ask clarifying questions until they understand what is being communicated? Well, this was one of those times.

"Which way should I turn it?" I ask, pointing to the left side of the rock. "Do you mean to turn the rock onto the left or the right side? Or, should I turn the rock upside down, or maybe instead of this being the front, should I turn it so the other side is facing out?"

"Right side down," she says. "It will look better that way."

I see what she is talking about. There is an interesting design on the rock's face, and turning it so the right side is down makes it look more distinctive.

This is one example among many years of seeing things from different points of view, different life experiences. Instead of arguing about who was right or who had the better idea, we focused on what we were working on. We are a team working on the end goal.

Yes, we frustrate each other. Yes, we both want to be right. I have found over the years that more often than not, we are both right. It comes down to a degree of rightness and what is best for that situation.

I have also learned that far more often than I like, I have been proven wrong. I am wrong about things I thought I was right about for sure. There is no need to be upset when this happens. Learn the new information and move on with your life. You now know more than you did. That's life. We learn as we go.

We are not perfect. We have our arguments. There is no yelling. We do not fight. We disagree. Sometimes we need to take some time to distance ourselves from the argument.

The thing I really love about this relationship is that we both know we are in it together. We are solid. We do not tiptoe around each other. We are not afraid to talk about the difficult things. That doesn't make the discussion easy. It is still a difficult discussion. We know that no matter what, we are partners and we are in it together.

You deserve a partner in all ways. Good relationships take work. They take open communication. They take sacrifice. They take understanding. They take empathy.

Good relationships give so much more. You are partners. You give to each other because it is the right thing to do. You want to be a better person because your partner deserves the best of you. You do it for them and become so much better for it. You each become better together than you ever could be apart.

Everyone deserves this type of understanding and respect in all the wonderful variations that are out there. I hope you continue to make your relationship the best it can be. If you are not in it yet, I hope you find it soon.

I hope you all find a partner like mine. I hope you do everything you can to become the best partner you can be.

Love is like a bird in a tree.
If you hold too tightly, it will flee.
Open your hands and let it go.
If true, it will stay and forever grow.
T. L. Scott

<u>Chapter 5: Debt Management.</u>

It is okay to be in debt. It is commendable to be debt-free. Neither is ideal when in excess. I admit that this is a somewhat unusual statement. Think about it, though. Obviously, if you are drowning in debt and you don't have two nickels to rub together, it is a problem. If you are midway through your pay period and don't know how you will make it to the end, it is a problem. If you are thinking about which bill to let slide this month so you can eat, you are in trouble. If you are in a relationship, then your partner is in trouble as well. Even if you are not in a relationship right now, those around you are affected. They see what is going on with you. They worry about you. They want you to succeed.

If this is you, stop right here. Seriously, do not do anything else. You need help, and you need it now. You should consult a professional financial counselor and lay out your finances to them so you can work together to develop a realistic plan to get out of this situation.

Ignoring it will not make it better. You must make a change. If you don't, things will get much worse. The factors that came together to result in your current circumstances will continue on the same trajectory if you do not introduce a change.

Being late or missing a month of payments can create a snowball effect: you will be hit with late and reactivation fees, your credit will suffer, and any loans you apply for will now be at a higher interest rate. That all results in you having even less money available. This is a downward spiral that only escalates. You have to stop it right now!

There really is no time to waste. These problems do not fix themselves. It takes a concentrated and dedicated effort to make things change. It won't be easy, but you CAN do it.

It's time for you to use that spreadsheet and put in your expenses. It is time to see where your money is really going.

Don't forget to check each of your credit accounts and see what interest you're paying each month. Take a hard look at that number. Deduct that number from the amount you paid for that month, and see clearly how much of your debt you paid that month.

Do that for each of your accounts, then add it all together. How much interest in total are you paying per month? How much of your money is really going to pay down your debt? Figure out those percentages. Do you like what you see?

Are you ready to change the dynamic from paying that much in interest to actually having your money make money for you?

The first step is getting your debt under control. Then we will get into how your money can make money for you.

Go ahead and use your trusty bookmark. I will be right here when you get back.

If you are debt-free, you would think you are doing well. This may not be the case, either. If you don't put yourself out there and use credit, you won't build a credit history.

I know we all know this, but let's put it front and center, shall we? Why do creditors, including credit card companies, loan you money? They do it to make money. It's simple. We all know this. We take it so much for granted that we don't even think about it.

As Americans, we have become a credit-based society. We buy our car with a loan. We put gas in the car's tank using a credit card. We go to the grocery store and buy our food with that credit card. We pay for everything with our credit card. We are a credit-based society.

That is how the banks and credit card companies make their money. They loan the money to you with a promise that you will pay them back. You will pay back what you borrowed, called the principal, at a fee called the interest rate. It is that interest rate that makes the bank its money.

The less risk they have in loaning you money, the more likely you are to pay them back, and the lower the interest rate. If they determine you are a higher-risk applicant due to a poor or limited credit history, they will loan you the money at a higher interest rate. Sadly, but understandably, those assessed at higher rates are the people who can least afford them. Those higher rates cost you more money for the same things.

When I bought my first car, I didn't know any of this. Nobody told me. I was young. I was confident. I didn't need to ask anybody for advice. I had money, and I wanted a car. I had a steady paycheck coming in. I had no worries. I really wish I had talked with someone who knew more than I did at the time.

I had gone past the dealerships for weeks. Their lots were full of clean, shiny, cool cars of all styles. I wandered the lot checking out the new models. In only a matter of minutes, one of the salespeople started talking with me.

In no time at all, we were moving from the new-car section to the used-car section. This guy knew what he was doing. I was not his first customer. I probably was not his first customer of the day. He was good at his job, and I must have been as easy to read as the dealership sign at the front of the lot.

Before long, I was sold on a sporty-looking car with low mileage. We went into the dealership to work out the sale. That was when a very difficult paradox confronted me. You see, I didn't have any credit. I had never bought anything on credit. I had never needed to. Now that I did, I realized I didn't have credit and couldn't get any because I didn't have a credit history.

Fortunately for me (more for him and his partner), he told me that he might know a way around this conundrum. We took a ride to a partner financial company that helped out people in my situation. He was able to give me a loan at a rate I could afford to pay back monthly. I was excited. I was able to buy my first car all on my own.

I wish I had paid attention to the interest rate. I was focused on the monthly cost instead. That short-sighted focus cost me a lot of money over time. I agreed to a loan at an annual percentage rate of 24.65 percent. I paid the loan off over time, a four-year loan.

Yes, I ended up paying over $8,000.00 for that $4,499.00 car.

I really loved that car and never regretted buying it. I very much regretted taking the loan that I did. I made a mistake then. I don't want anyone to make the same mistake I did.

I strongly advise you to visit your bank or credit union before visiting a car dealership. Yes, that includes online shopping as well. Discuss with your bank or credit union the options available to you based on your financial situation. This way, you will know where you stand before you ever come face-to-face with a salesperson.

You will know how much you can really afford because you have already been pre-approved for that amount and know how much the loan will cost you. You will be able to compare the loan rate to what you were offered by your bank or credit union and determine whether it is a better deal.

Knowing this will put you in a much better bargaining position. Let's look at a scenario you may face.

You are considering buying a car. If you buy a $30,000 car at 8 percent interest for a loan with a payback over five years, how much would you pay in interest? You would end up paying $6,497.51. That is almost 21.7 percent of the car's total cost. Your car payment would be $608.29 per month.

Now, let's say you decide to lower the monthly payment to make it more affordable. If you made the loan for six years instead of five, the monthly payment would decrease to a more manageable $526.00. The problem is that even if the interest rate remains at 8 percent, your total interest payments increase to $7,871.80. You are paying 26.24 percent more for the car. You get the convenience of paying over time, but make no mistake, you are paying for that convenience.

When talking with these sales agents, remember that it is their job to sell. It is your job to make the best deal for yourself. They are counting on you wanting that new shiny thing. While you are feeling those happy feelings and your body is swimming in endorphins, those sales agents are presenting you with options and extended warranties. Restrain yourself! Your job is to get the best deal for yourself. Not all of the things being offered are the best deal for you. Take a breath. Take emotion out of it. Be analytical. Be ready to walk away if they are not ready to make the best deal for you. Other places are selling that exact make and model of vehicle. You may find a better deal elsewhere.

Do your research first on what you need in your vehicle, so you don't get pressured into options you don't need. Be practical and get the best out of the deal that you can. Be prepared. Be knowledgeable. Know where you stand financially.

Most people do not have the $30,000.00 free to go pay up front for their car. Credit is good if you manage it well. The lower risk you pose to the lender, the better rate you will get on a loan, and the less you will pay for the convenience of using credit. You will get the vehicle you want, with the options you want, at a lower cost to you when all is said and done.

How do you get there?

Establishing a solid credit history is one of the most important things you can do. A large part of that is demonstrating fiscal responsibility.

Looking back at my mistake when buying my first car, it is easy to see that I would have significantly benefited from shopping around. If I hadn't been so impulsive and had been more methodical, it would have cost me much less over time. That salesman knew that and took advantage of it. Businesses today do the same thing. Look at the payment structure for places like Rent-A-Center and Rooms to Go. They are designed to satisfy your short-term need/want by showing you a smaller weekly payment for what you want. Take the time and calculate the total cost of the item over time to see what kind of "deal" you are really signing up for.

Take a breath.

Take a minute and step back.

Take note of the base price and the total final price over time.

With a smile on your face, tell the sales agent you plan to shop at a few more retailers and that you will keep their offer in mind. Know that these sales agents are likely working on commission, so it is in their best interest to close the sale with you and not have you walk out the door. Nothing against them or that business structure. It's just probably not in your best long-term fiscal interest to do business that way.

Go to the other store. See what they have to offer. They might offer you a 0 percent interest deal if you pay within a certain period of time. This is a great offer if you pay it off within that period. It is in the company's best interest when customers do not pay it off within that time and are then assessed all the interest that is due. If you choose this deal, make sure you pay it off on time!

The main point is to avoid impulse buying. Be methodical with your financial decisions. Pause for a minute and ask whether you really need it or just want it. Can you do without it? Can it wait until you have saved up for it? When you pay cash or have the cash to pay off the credit card charge before the end of the statement period, then you only pay the base price with no interest. Look at it as if you are saving that money.

Let's get back to the conundrum of needing credit but not having credit. We must show creditors that we can be trusted so that we are easily approved when we apply for a car or truck loan. When we eventually apply for a home mortgage, we are approved.

We don't want to only be approved. We want to be approved at the lowest possible interest rate. The way to do that is to have a high credit rating. How do we do that? Great question. I am so happy you asked. Ready? This is a roadmap to follow.

If you have a steady income stream, such as a paycheck, your financial institution will likely approve your credit card application. It probably will not be for a very high credit limit, and it will likely be at a higher interest rate than you want.

This is all manageable. You really don't want a high credit limit. It is too easy to tell yourself that you have money available. I want to be very clear about that. You do not have money available. You have credit available, and that credit costs you money. Pause and think about that.

The thing about credit cards is that if you pay off the balance before the end of the statement cycle, you do not pay any interest on purchases. Nothing! Zero! Nada!

If you happen to have a credit card that offers cash back and you pay it off before the end of the payment cycle, you'll have zero interest and receive free money to help you pay off that amount. How cool is that?

The thing is that these financial institutions know that most people do not exercise such discipline. They do not pay off their balance monthly. They let it accumulate. They make the minimum payment due. They run up the balance across multiple cards. Many people are struggling with debt due to high interest rates.

Do not let this be you. I admit it has been me. I let myself fall into the trap of making minimum payments. I was counting the days to the next paycheck so I could cover the bills. All the while I was looking at the short term, those interest rates were adding up. I was making the payment. I was getting by. But I was paying the company more and more the longer I kept doing this. I finally had enough and made up my mind to do something about it.

If this is you, or if you see yourself becoming this person, you can do something about it. Let's go.

Time To Take Control

Let's start at the beginning, fiscally speaking. It is payday. Yay! Time to go and have fun.

Take a breath. No, really… take a breath. Just relax for a second and put things into perspective. Slow it down a little. There, now let's talk about goals and how to get there.

You have to have discipline to get to where you want to be. The first step is to know what is going on with your money. So, your money just came in. From that amount, sit down and review what you owe. What are your bills? Let's look at the minimum payment amounts. I stress the word minimum! Where is your money going, and how much will you have after you pay for everything? Minimum payments only at this point. Begin with the larger payments, like your rent, mortgage, car payment, and child care, and move on to the smaller payments from there, like your insurance and individual utility bills.

Keep doing this with all of your regular payments, including your credit cards. Document the minimum payment due.

Now let's look at how much you paid for gas last month. Easy to do. Just look at your previous credit card statement. This isn't the only way. Maybe you used your debit card for those transactions. There are advantages to either approach, which we will discuss in the following pages. Surprisingly, Americans spend over $2,000.00 a month on gas, according to the Energy Information Administration.

Now do the same for groceries and all of the other things you bought last month. It is time to figure out how much money you will have available when everything is said and done. Your results will vary, but I bet it is less than you thought you had available at the end of the month.

Here is a quick example using conservative numbers:

Financial Tracker			
Annual Gross Pay	Net Pay	Monthly Pay	Paycheck
$65,000.00	$40,000.00	$3,333.00	$1,666.50

This is only a simple example. Let's say your gross pay is around $65,000 a year. Congratulations, your take-home pay each month is $3,333 or $1,650.00 per paycheck every two weeks. Remember, this is your take-home pay, or your net pay. This is what is left after your taxes, Medicare, Medicaid, 401(k), health insurance, dental insurance, and retirement are deducted.

So, you bring home $3,333.00 per month, and your initial bills total $2,358.00 per month.

Payment	Date	Amount	Declining Balance
Rent	5th	$900.00	$2,433.00
Electricity	5th	$150.00	$2,283.00
Garbage	5th	$20.00	$2,263.00
TV Cable	16th	$80.00	$2,183.00
Streaming	17th	$48.00	$2,135.00
Internet	18th	$85.00	$2,050.00
Car Payment	19th	$750.00	$1,300.00
Insurance	20th	$175.00	$1,125.00
Phone	20th	$150.00	$975.00
		$2,358.00	**$975.00**
		Total Spent	**Remaining Balance**

Congratulations, you still have $975.00. Oh, wait, we didn't account for your consumables:

Payment	Amount	Balance
Gas	$150.00	$825.00
Groceries	$350.00	$475.00
Restaurant	$200.00	$275.00
Entertainment	$100.00	$175.00
Clothes	$100.00	$75.00
Miscellaneous	$75.00	**$0.00**

We now have a problem. With that reasonable spending we are out of money. What about those credit cards? What was the balance on them? What is the minimum monthly payment? We have a problem.

Now it is time for you to work out your own financial picture. I recommend setting up an Excel spreadsheet. There are many free templates and other resources available online, such as this one:

Simple-Excel-Budget-Template.xlsx

This process doesn't have to be complicated, but if you're into that, then go for complicated. You can color-code, create tabs, use pivot tables, extrapolate, and project to your heart's content.

The next step is to determine where the other money has gone. A good way to do this is to go to your bank statement from ideally six months ago. If you can't go back that far, three months will give you a good financial picture. Track each paycheck as it comes in and document all withdrawals for the month. Know where that money went. If there are cash withdrawals, try to account for where the cash went.

After you know where the money has gone from your bank accounts, go to your credit card account. Document the transactions on that card and any other cards you have.

Put all those transactions into the spreadsheet—all of it. Do not hide anything. You will only be hurting yourself.

Go over your known bills and make sure they are all accounted for: everything from grocery bills to ordering food delivery to your morning coffee. Account for every penny if possible. Don't forget about your subscriptions. Those can add up quickly, too.

Deduct all these expenditures from the incoming revenue stream. This assessment should help you see clearly where your money is going. If you do not like the bottom-line numbers after each paycheck or at the end of the month, ask yourself whether there are areas you can cut back on. Do you have memberships you pay for but do not use? Could you save some money by bringing your coffee with you to work instead of buying it on the way? Maybe pack your lunch a few times a week instead of grabbing fast food?

Another thing to look at is the interest rate on your credit cards. You may be surprised by their current rates. You should target the ones with the higher rates first and pay down/pay off their debt as aggressively as you can.

You may also want to look at debt consolidation. Some credit cards offer low to no interest rates to consolidate debt from other cards onto that one. Pay particular attention to the terms for this. Know the period offered for the low rate and what happens if the amount isn't paid off within that period. Are there any costs associated with this consolidation? How much will it save you after you pay the costs? How much will it cost you to leave things as they are? Really put in the work and find out what is best for you.

Once you make your decision, be disciplined about it. If you decide to cut back in specific areas, then follow through and do that. If you plan to pay off a specific card aggressively and not make any more charges to it, follow through with that plan.

The first rule to follow is that credit is not free money.

The second rule is that having available credit does not mean you have available money to spend. If you break this rule, you will quickly find yourself in trouble.

Do you like living paycheck to paycheck? Are you able to manage a major repair to your car without extending your credit load? What if you were to become suddenly unemployed? How long could you hold out? You need a plan.

When I was young and making my way, I wish someone had offered me some financial guidance. I wish I had sought it out, but I did not. I will share with you one of the things I really regret doing.

I was a young parent, a single parent with two young children, trying to make ends meet. I take my hat off to all parents out there, especially those of you who are doing it on your own.

Being a parent is hard in the best of times. Juggling all the daily activities that need to be managed to keep a household running, while somehow finding ways to pay for it all. Life is not cheap. Raising children is really not cheap. Paying for childcare, diapers, formula, groceries, clothes, and the hundreds of other things that need to be paid for and taken care of can be a big drain on one's finances. To those of you raising children, I salute you one and all.

In my struggles to stretch my finances to the next paycheck, I, at times, engaged in what is called floating checks. I don't think it's possible now, but back then it would take three to five days for a check to clear and for the money to be deducted from your account.

Knowing this, I would write a check for cash to cover the things I needed. Then, every two days, I would repeat the process and deposit the money into the checking account to cover the next check that would be deducted from the account. When payday hit, the money was there to cover the transactions. But I was playing with fire. If I miscalculated and missed a transaction, the check could bounce, incurring extra costs, as I did not have the money to cover it.

I didn't do this often, and I am glad it was only for a brief period. I justified it to myself as something I needed to do. The truth was that I really didn't need to do it. What I needed to do was manage my finances so that I didn't need to do it at all.

Remember the car loan I took out at just under 25 percent interest? That extra money I gave to that finance company would have been nice for me to have. Remember when I mentioned Rent-A-Center and similar companies? I wish I had known better and not spent the extra money then. I wish I knew then what I am sharing with you now.

Be patient! You did not get yourself into this situation overnight, and you won't get out of it overnight.

Once you get your financial house in order, what's next?

First of all, congratulations! Celebrate that achievement, and think back to how it felt when you decided to make this change. Remember how frustrated and out of control you felt? Promise yourself that you'll never allow it to happen again.

It is generally agreed that you should have three to six months of earnings readily available in case of emergencies. I imagine you don't think you can do that. It's a lot of money. Yes, it is a lot. You won't get there quickly, but you can get there. It takes time, planning, and a whole lot of discipline.

Readily available does not mean to stash it under your mattress. I don't recommend you leave it in a savings or checking account either. Look at the rate of return for those savings and checking accounts at the bank or credit union, and you will see what I mean. But rest assured that it is indeed safe, as the FDIC protects it for banks and the NCUSIF protects it for credit unions up to $250,000.00 per depositor.

Instead of limiting yourself to savings and checking accounts, look at certificates of deposit. Most financial institutions have them, and some offer higher rates than others. Shop around for the best deal for you. These CDs have different terms. Some are offered for three, six, or 12 months. Others are for multiple years. The advantage of these investment vehicles is that you can access your money if you need it in a relatively short period of time while still earning a higher return.

- Get your financial house in order.
- Be disciplined.
- Be patient.
- Is it a want or is it a need?
- Stick with your plan.
- Live your life, be wise in your choices.
- Have a financial plan.
- Save for specific things or events.
- Invest in yourself.
- Invest in your future.

I will review my financial situation by:______________

I will increase my payments for:________________

To pay it off by:________________

I will be debt free by:__________________

Chapter 6: Investments

In the previous chapter, we touched on investing. We talked a little about savings and checking accounts, as well as certificates of deposit (CDs). We discussed getting your financial affairs in order and then creating a plan for your future.

In this chapter, we are going to go into more detail about other ways to invest your money. You owe it to yourself to become knowledgeable about the various investment tools available and their advantages and risks. Yes, there are risks.

You have to determine the level of risk you are comfortable taking and weigh the risks, your aversion to or acceptance of those risks, and the immediacy of your goals.

Let's say you are completely averse to taking risks. The mere thought of risk makes you nervous. You decide to keep your money safe. You withdraw your money from the bank and stuff it into your mattress.

Obviously, if someone breaks into your home and steals your money, you have problems. Will your homeowners' or renters' insurance cover that loss? It is a risk.

Let's say you decide to leave your money in the bank in a savings account. Look at your own financial institution for its rates. A quick online search reveals a range from 0.004 percent to 4.5 percent under certain conditions. Hey, 4.5 percent doesn't sound bad, right?

Now we need to look at another factor. What is the inflation rate? The definition I found on NerdWallet states that inflation is the rate at which the prices of goods and services increase. As a result of inflation, the purchasing power (value) of money decreases over time. Inflation affects the prices of everything around us.

Now that we have a definition of inflation, we need to know how much it is. According to the Bureau of Labor Statistics, the inflation rate for the previous 12 months, ending March 31, 2024, was 3.5 percent.

So, that money you stuffed inside your mattress, if it didn't get stolen, depreciated in value by 3.5 percent. If you have savings in a high-yield savings account, it might have gained 1 percent.

Let's take a closer look at inflation. Let's say you purchased something for $100.00 five years ago. Based on an annual inflation rate of 2.5 percent, that same item would now cost you $122.21. If you were not to buy that item and leave the $100.00 in your savings account, it would now be worth $105.10, considering an average rate of return of 1 percent.

Now, let's assume you put the same $100.00 into an investment account with an annual rate of return of 6 percent. That same $100.00 would be worth $133.82.

Let that sink in for a minute. If you do not stay ahead of inflation, you are losing money. The average inflation rate has been 2.5 percent. The average annual rate of return for the stock market over the past 50 years has been 9.4 percent.

What are we talking about? What are these investing tools? I am confident you are familiar with savings and checking accounts. I will briefly describe them here.

A checking account allows you to write paper checks against the money you have in your account. You can also use your debit card to function like a credit card without any interest being accrued against you, as the funds are immediately deducted from your checking account. These accounts are primarily used to make your frequent payments. Some banks and credit unions charge fees and require minimum balances. Check with your financial institution to compare your rates.

Savings accounts are designed for account holders to hold their funds and receive a specific amount of interest on them. Check your account to see your rate of return.

One reason the rate of return on checking accounts is typically lower than that on savings accounts is the anticipated higher turnover in checking accounts. Most people do not leave large amounts of money in these accounts that build over time.

If you are leaving your money in your savings account, return to the beginning of this chapter and review the interest on your current savings account. Go ahead and calculate how much that decision is costing you. If you are making a profit and feel safe with it, then you do you. Here are some other options for you to consider.

People do place their money in Certificates of Deposit. These investment tools are designed for specific periods and have set rates of return. Typically, the longer the term, the higher the rate of return.

An example is purchasing a $500.00 CD for a three-month term at 4 percent interest. At the end of the three months, they will have earned $4.93. If they take that same $500 and buy a 12-month CD at 4 percent, they will have $20.00. Now, think about this for a minute, if you will.

What if you did that every year? Take that $500.00, plus the $20.00 in interest, and buy another CD for 12 months, adding $500.00 to it each year.

I am sure you can see how it can grow considerably over time. Let's make it more fun. What if you invest $100.00 out of each paycheck? Assume you get paid twice a month, which is equivalent to 24 investments of $100.00 each. If you invested $2,400.00 in that first year, you would earn approximately $96.00 just by using your money.

Pay Day	Month	Yr	Interest	Total
$100.00	$200.00	$2,400.00	$96.00	$2,496.00

Now, let's say you take that $2,496.00 and buy yourself a five-year CD.

The first year, your $2,496.00 earns 4 percent.

On the anniversary, you add $2,400.00 to that $2,496.00, plus the 4 percent earned through that year, and you have $5,091.84. Do the same on the second anniversary, and your investment is now $7,791.58. Each year it continues to grow. At the end of the five-year term, you have $16,555.91. That is only $100.00 from each paycheck, or $10.00 per workday. You can do this!

	Beginning Balance	Annual Deposit	Interest Earned	Year End Balance
Initial Yr	$2,496.00	$2,400.00	$195.84	$5,091.84
2nd Yr	$5,091.84	$2,400.00	$299.67	$7,791.51
3rd Yr	$7,791.51	$2,400.00	$407.66	$10,599.17
4th Yr	$10,599.17	$2,400.00	$519.97	$13,519.14
5th Yr	$13,519.14	$2,400.00	$636.77	$16,555.91

I am sure you see the power in this. Each subsequent year, your money earns you more money at that interest rate. As long as you reinvest it, your earnings are compounded. When you do this, you are using compound interest to your advantage. You are letting your money grow. You are building your wealth.

I want to be very clear here. Your level of risk when your money is in the bank or credit union, whether in a savings or checking account, Certificates of Deposit, or other internal investment tools, is insured up to $250,000.00.

This is not the case for investments that are traded on the stock market. This includes banks or credit unions that offer investment services. That insurance does not cover your investments in the stock market. If you have questions about this, I encourage you to reach out to your bank, credit union, or investment service, and to conduct your own research.

You can also purchase Savings Bonds and other types of bonds. The U. S. Government backs savings bonds. Basically, you are loaning your money to the government. EE bonds are sold at face value and guaranteed to double in value in 20 years. Another type of savings bond is the Series I bond. The Series I has a fixed interest rate plus an inflation rate that adjusts every six months. These are considered a safe investment option.

Other types of bonds include corporate bonds, treasury bonds, municipal bonds, and green bonds, which are designed to fund environmentally friendly projects. They all basically function in the same way in that you loan your money to the bondholder for a specific interest rate. These are considered safe investments, and you should learn more about them to determine if they are right for your investment strategy.

What is a stock, and what is the stock market? A stock is simply a share of a company. Those who own the shares are called shareholders. There are privately owned companies and publicly owned companies.

Privately owned companies are not traded on the stock exchanges. One or more people own them, but the public cannot purchase an interest or share in the company.

Public companies have their shares listed and are traded on the stock markets such as the New York Stock Exchange (NYSE) and the NASDAQ. These are where the majority of trades are conducted in America. Other countries also have their own exchanges.

You may come across stocks that are traded on the Open Market or the OTC. I encourage you to proceed with extreme caution with OTC-traded stocks. These are often referred to as penny stocks. They can be tempting. You can buy a large amount of shares for not a lot of money. The temptation, the possibility that the stock will climb up from, say, $00.0003 per share to $10.00, is powerful. You could make a large amount of money.

STOP!

There is a reason this company's shares are not listed on a major exchange. It could be that they are a small company and deserve a chance. It is possible. It is also probable that there is a reason they do not meet the listing requirements of the NASDAQ or the NYSE. These stocks should be viewed as extremely risky.

Believe me! I have been burned.

I ignored all of the warning signs, even when news hit the streets that this company's audit company, a major and well-respected company they had just hired, parted ways with them. I should have seen a big, neon flashing sign that said "Warning!" Warning! Big Problems Ahead!"

Me: Nope! This is an opportunity. This company is going to pull through it and make me even more money.

That is the problem with blind faith. I failed to separate my emotions from my analysis of the company's fundamentals. Seriously, their audit company identified so many problems that they dropped them as a client to avoid becoming embroiled in the issues they uncovered after gaining access to their records.

I was a believer, even when news reports emerged that the Securities and Exchange Commission (SEC) was investigating them. I finally sold my shares at a considerable loss, just before the news broke that the company's primary officers had been arrested. They were found guilty, and I lost my money.

Publicly owned companies are owned by the public through shares. Basically, the company receives money for these shares at a pre-determined amount per share. For example, let's say the company has been valued at $5 million and intends to offer 100,000 shares. This would place the value of each share at $50.00 for the initial public offering. That is what it is offered at initially. Depending on public interest, that price could, and often does, go up and down in value.

So, hypothetically, let's suppose you buy five shares at the initially offered price (IPO) of $50.00 per share. You spent $250.00 and now own five shares of this theoretical company. Say you are happy with how they do business and hold your shares for ten years. If the company's shares perform in line with the average historical return of the stock market and your investment increases at a 10 percent yearly rate, your five shares would have doubled in value and are now worth $500.00.

This is only an example, and the performance of any stock or company is subject to many factors. The value may increase or decrease dramatically. It is up to each investor to do their own research and determine the level of risk they are willing to take.

One way to mitigate some of this risk is by investing in mutual funds. You may have heard of these before. Mutual funds are essentially baskets of assets purchased by a fund manager and then overseen by that manager. These managers are responsible for understanding the details of their specific markets and the businesses in which they are invested. They truly are the professionals.

So, what is a mutual fund? Let's say you buy one share of Coca-Cola. What if Pepsi does better and the share price of Coca-Cola drops on you? That would be the risk you are taking. As a side note, both Coke and Pepsi are highly diversified companies that cover many market segments, not just soft drinks. They are both worth a look. In fact, both of these very large companies behave similarly to mutual funds on their own.

Back to a true mutual fund. These fund managers purchase shares of companies and add them to their investment portfolio. This portfolio is the focus for investments.

Let's say, for example, you want a mutual fund that has a focus on technology. You would research technology mutual funds. If you are looking for a safe, long-term fund, you could consider large-cap blue-chip funds that focus on companies with a long history, like IBM, Ford, 3M, and others. These large companies typically do not experience rapid growth. Their place in their market is well established. Their stock prices typically grow slowly. Their share prices also do not typically fall quickly.

If you are looking for companies that may be on the forefront of technological breakthroughs, then look to younger, startup companies with less capital, referred to as small-cap funds.

You can find and research mutual funds focused on the auto industry, health care, AI, robotics, technology, and more.

The diversity of mutual funds is great. So are the advantages of using them. Having an array of companies in a single portfolio spreads risk across multiple companies. If one company underperforms, the others may not. Also, the fund managers are professionals. They know what they are doing and can better assess risks than the average person. It is their job to know these companies and the markets in which they operate.

The average person does not have the time to conduct the research necessary to know these details as fund managers do. Do your research and find funds that align with your risk tolerance and have a strong track record of performance.

Another thing to consider when planning your investment strategy is dividends. As we have already covered, a stock's value fluctuates over time based on the company's perceived value. Ideally, that value increases over time, and your investment grows. Some companies also offer a dividend.

These large, well-established companies typically pay dividends. According to Investopedia, "A dividend is a distribution of a company's profits to its shareholders, typically paid out on a set schedule."

They distribute a portion of their profits back to their shareholders. This can range from 1.5 percent to 5.6 percent per share, for example. Typically, the lower the dividend, the lower the perceived risk.

If you come across a company that is offering a high dividend rate, you may be tempted to view it as a must-buy automatically. But pump those brakes, friends. Research is required.

Many factors go into determining the percentage the company will set for its dividend distributions, as well as how frequently it will pay dividends. Some pay dividends monthly, while others do it quarterly or even annually.

There may be a good reason for the dividend to be high, say 10 to 15 percent. Some companies are structured such that they are required to distribute their profits. Look into Real Estate Investment Trusts, or REITS. These can be good investment tools.

You can take those dividends and set them to be automatically reinvested. Every time the distribution is paid out, they buy more shares for you. By doing this, you avoid paying taxes on that dividend distribution.

If you hold a share for the long term, one year or more, you are taxed at a lower rate than if you sold it before the anniversary of your purchase. It is recommended that you hold your stocks for the long term. Not only will you realize a lower tax rate on your eventual sale, but you will also hopefully be able to sell for a profit from the company performing well over time. Remember, the average return of the stock market is gauged over time. You need to own your stock long enough to realize those average returns.

Do your best to make your financial decisions analytically. Separate these decisions from your emotions. People tend to become tied to their decisions. They believe they were right in their choice.

If they hold onto their investment a little longer, the company will turn things around. I fell into this trap and lost quite a bit on that bad decision. Reader beware. For a tale of caution, read into the case of the little company called Sponge Tech.

The Spongetech CEO and CFO Settle with the SEC – SEC ACTIONS

Please do better than I did then. Do your research. Read the financial reports about the company. If the analysts are recommending a sell rating, you should pay attention. On the other hand, just because an analyst gives a stock a buy rating, it doesn't mean you should invest all your money into it. Do your research. Analyze the company. Analyze the industry. Read the news. Be informed. Do not let emotions guide your investments.

One way you can minimize your risk is to place a floor on your stock. Basically, set up a standing order that if the share price falls to a preset limit, the system triggers a sale. You can determine how many of your shares are included in this action. You can also do it the other way. If the share price climbs to a level you like, you can set up your account to trigger a sale, thereby locking in your hoped-for gains.

You can also do this to buy shares. Say you see the share price is at $25.04 and you want to buy some shares. You have done your research and see a trend: typically, in the days leading up to the earnings report, the price tends to go down. You want to take advantage of this and place an order to buy your shares at $24.75. If the price goes down that much, it will trigger your purchase. Hopefully, the earnings report will be positive, and the share price will go up again.

Another emotional pitfall to be aware of is called sunk costs. This is when an investor has put their money into a company and is not willing to sell and cut their losses. They look at past performance and hope, wish, believe that the company will turn things around.

That was me once upon a time. It stinks! It hurts! Take your emotions out of it. What does your research tell you to do? Take your losses and sell it. Move your money into another investment that your research shows will do well.

In the course of your investment education, you will likely learn about puts and calls. Some people have great success with these. They invest their time in thoroughly researching companies and market trends. They treat these activities as a business.

Most people do not have the time to thoroughly educate themselves about the potential companies, let alone the industry and the stock market in general. They do not dedicate their time to scanning financials for what analysts are saying, tracking news sources, or combing through companies' financial statements to determine which to buy and which to sell based on market forecasts of ups and downs. I will not go into any more detail on puts and calls here. It is more complicated and requires a more detailed discussion than I want to go into in this book.

If you are interested in learning more, you can look at Investopedia or many other sites. A simple search in your search engine will provide good results. Please do not just look at the first result. Do a little research and arm yourself with knowledge. If you choose to do so, be educated and be thorough. I wish you well.

You work hard for your money. Be careful with it. Let your money grow over time. Restrain yourself from getting caught up in impulse buying. Try to research as much as possible before you decide to purchase or invest in something. Refrain from dipping into your investments as much as possible. Let your gains compound over time.

If you do not have a 401 (k) through your employer, and they offer one, you should take advantage of it. First off, your contributions are not taxed. This immediately saves you money. Come tax time, your adjusted gross earnings will have gone down. Translation: You will probably pay less annual taxes or get a larger tax return. Some employers match their employees' contributions to their 401 (k) up to a set amount. If they do this, why would you turn down free money?

A 401 (k) is basically a mutual fund that allows contributions to be tax-deferred. The taxes come when you withdraw the money, hopefully during your retirement years. You will likely earn less and pay a lower tax rate.

Let's say your company does not offer a 401 (k). Where do you turn? Look no further than the Individual Retirement Account, or IRA for short. You can also get into an IRA if you have a 401 (k).

There are two types of IRAs: Roth and traditional. The main difference is that with a Roth IRA, you pay taxes on the money you invest, and when you take distributions from the IRA, the taxes have already been paid. The Traditional IRA functions much like the 401 (k) in that the money invested is tax-deferred and can reduce your adjusted gross earnings. You will pay tax on your distributions when you withdraw them from the IRA.

Another investment option is cryptocurrency. This is a new investment option. Remember when I talked about the bank and credit union insuring your investments? This is nothing like it.

When you invest in stocks, you are buying a share of a company. The investment is based on something. If you are interested in investing in cryptocurrency, know that you are not really investing in anything. The currency is not based on anything more than speculation.

That said, people are making profits from their crypto investments. People are also losing money on their crypto investments. I will include a link to cryptocurrencies in the references section if you want to start there and learn more. Please do learn more about them before you decide to invest your hard-earned money in them.

Do your research, no matter where you intend to invest your money. You work very hard. Make your money work for you.

You have options. I strongly encourage you to learn about these options and take advantage of them. The earlier you do so, the better for your fiscal well-being. You must decide on the course of action that is best for you. The best action for you may change over time. The more you know about your options, the better prepared you are to manage those decision points.

Knowledge is power. More knowledge makes you more powerful. Arm yourself. You never know when or what kind of battle you will face.

I will monthly invest: $___________

Name the stock, ETF, CD, etc. ___________

What is a long-term goal you want to invest/save for?_________________________________

How much will it cost?_________________

What is your plan?_____________________

Chapter 7: Never Stop Learning

"Once you stop learning, you start dying."
Albert Einstein

As a writer, I frequently engage people in discussions. One question I ask is whether they enjoy reading. When I first started asking this question, I was surprised by how many people readily said they don't read. This prompted me to check whether this response was just random or, in fact, whether many people do not read. I did a quick internet search and found that 33 percent of high school graduates never read another book after graduation.

I have come to find that there are many reasons people do not read. I am not judging. I was just surprised. Because I love to read so much, I assumed most people did as well. We are all different, though, so everyone should do what is right for them.

Whether it is through reading, watching videos, or listening to audiobooks, I strongly encourage everyone to continue learning. Learn about whatever it is you are interested in. Learn about how to invest, as we discussed in the previous chapter. Learn about how to build a birdhouse. Learn about how to be more assertive at work. Learn how to be a better communicator. Yeah, that is one we should all work on.

We all need to continue learning. We all need to become better at what we do. We need to learn how to do new things and how to handle the challenges we face.

For example, there are many books out there on how to be a good parent. No one is a perfect parent. We can all do better. Don't have any little ones at home? Be a better grandparent. Be a better aunt or uncle. Be a better you. Learn how to do that.

If you want to go back to school and get your college degree, I encourage you to go for it. If you want to get your postgraduate degree, then that is what you should do. If you want to get a certification in a completely different field, then do that!

Don't let anyone tell you that you can't.

I want you to think about this. When a person is telling you that you cannot do something, more often than not, what they are really telling you is that they don't believe they could do it. They are judging you based on their own limitations, which are often self-imposed. Do not let them define you.

Do not be your own worst enemy. Do not listen when your doubts crowd in. Don't talk your way out of giving it a shot.

Until you have given your best effort, you do not know whether you can or cannot. Take your shot. Work for it. If you don't succeed, then reassess and re-engage. Find another way to get to that goal. If you need more time, then give yourself more time. If you need more money, then find a way to budget for it. There are many paths to success. Not trying will lead you nowhere. Not risking failure will ensure you will not improve. Give it your best. You will be surprised by just how much you can achieve when you are focused on growing.

I recently watched an interview with Neil DeGrasse Tyson in which he shared a story about his father. When his dad was young, he was told he could not be a runner because he didn't have the right build. Not only did he disregard that classification, but he also used it to motivate himself.

He refused to allow another person to define what he could or could not do. He trained and worked hard until he became a great runner. He actually became a world-class athlete. I encourage you to look up the story of Cyril deGrasse Tyson. It is a very motivating example. He was a sociologist and served as the

Human Resources Commissioner for New York City. He was also the first director of Harlem Youth Opportunities Unlimited.

I have heard too many people tell me that they are not good learners. I respond with this: Maybe you were not interested in learning about that particular topic. If you want to learn something, then get to it.

Do not ever tell yourself you can't. You can! More than that, you need to.

You *need* to feed that curiosity. You *need* to feed that desire to become better. You *need* to continue challenging yourself to improve and learn continuously.

Seriously, you would not be reading these words if you did not want to improve. You would not have invested your time and effort to get to this point in the book unless you recognized this desire inside of yourself.

You feel the pull to do something more, something better than what you have been doing. You feel a pull to become more than you are today.

It is time for that change.

Is there a hobby or interest you have always wanted to try?_______________________________

What is holding you back?_________________

Go for it!

Is there something you have wanted to know more about? _______________________________

The information is readily available to you.

I will begin learning it by:_______________

<u>Chapter 8: Challenge Yourself</u>

While I was in the early stages of writing this book, I was trying to isolate the lessons I wanted to share with you. I had a good idea of what they would be, but I didn't want to overlook something because I hadn't thought of it.

Despite my best efforts, I am sure there are subjects I have not included in this book. Let me know what you want to know more about, and I will include it in the next book.

Excuse me, I digress. So, I was researching topics to write about, to share with you. I decided to tap into my local knowledge base. I asked readers like you what they would like to know more about. Unsurprisingly, most people did not know what to say.

One of the most intelligent people I know shared a phrase with me that I repeat frequently now. "You don't know what you don't know." Wait, what?

I recall a commercial from a while back in which the actor discussed the need to borrow something as a new homeowner. He said he had to ask his neighbor to borrow a pole saw. He had never heard of a pole saw before. He didn't know what one was, let alone that he would need one, until he was presented with a situation where it was the right tool for the job.

"You don't know what you don't know."

That is okay. No, that is really a great thing. As much as you know, and I am going to assume that you know a great deal about many things, there are many more things we know nothing about.

We all have much more to learn. It takes effort, though. We are all busy. There is always something we need to do, and at the end of the day, we deserve a rest, right?

Yes! We all deserve a rest.

Be very careful!

Sir Isaac Newton's first law of motion describes the property of inertia, which defines the resistance objects have to changes in their motion, whether that change is to speed up or slow down the object, or to change its direction. All objects of mass will continue to move at a constant speed, in the same direction, unless acted upon by an outside force. If an object of mass is not moving, it will stay at rest unless pushed or pulled by an outside force.

Why in the world am I bringing physics into this? It is primarily because of the last sentence. Basically, objects in motion stay in motion, and objects at rest remain at rest. The same applies to each of us. It takes effort to move us into a state of change. To continue propelling ourselves along that path of change, we have to keep pushing. We must continue to strive for improvement.

When we get into the habit of relaxing too much and taking it too easy, it becomes increasingly difficult to break out of that pattern. Newton explained it. Actual forces are pushing you to stay where you are. Change takes effort. It is not easy. It is also not impossible.

Picture this with me. As you recall, I am an old salt. During my time in the Navy, I was stationed on four different ships. I can tell you for sure that big changes do not happen all at once. Turning a ship is not an immediate thing. It turns by degrees. It takes time. Change, well, most intentional change takes time. These changes are rarely the result of a single action. Numerous small actions lead to and result in the overall change.

The same applies to your efforts. You cannot pay off all your debt with your next paycheck. You didn't get into your current condition that quickly. Why would you believe you can get out of it quickly? It will take work. It will take small adjustments over time. When you achieve that goal and look back, you will see that those minor corrections led you to your success. Picture a ship doing minor course corrections to sail a smooth course.

The same process goes into everything else. When you begin studying a new course, you read the first word of the first sentence of the first paragraph of the first chapter. Your efforts build upon your previous efforts.

After I retired from the Navy, I relaxed. I didn't have to pass PT tests anymore. Nobody was checking whether I met the height/weight standards. I let my hair grow out. I tried growing a beard.

My beard didn't last long. I didn't feel comfortable with it.

I cut my hair before it got too long, too. After 24 years, I had grown accustomed to being clean-shaven and having short hair. Even to this day, I keep my hair and my beard short.

I got to a point where I was not comfortable with my weight. I did not like my level of physical fitness. I was breathing too hard for doing so little. I made an intentional change. I began running again.

It was frustrating. My mind said I could run like I used to. My body was not cooperating. I couldn't catch my breath. I struggled to run 1 mile before stopping. And that was at a very slow pace.

I kept at it, though. I built up my strength. I built up my endurance. I built up my inner determination. I was making the effort. My determination pushed back against those forces trying to keep me from moving. My discipline kept me doing it day after day, week after week.

I began running races. Me against the course and the clock. I was focused on my own improvement. I ran some 5Ks, then some 10Ks. I really liked those distances. They were short enough that I could take them on and push through them.

I decided to push harder and took on the half-marathon challenge. I can tell you from personal experience that the half-marathon is not the same as those shorter distances. I found that it took more mental discipline to keep pushing to complete the 13.1 miles.

After doing a few of those halfs, I looked ahead to the next logical challenge—the marathon, 26.2 miles. I thought about it for quite a while. I kept doing the halfs while telling myself I was training. It was true. I was training. I was also holding myself back from taking on the challenge of running 26.2 miles.

By this time, I was approaching a significant milestone in my life. I was going to turn 50 in a couple of years. I made up my mind. I was going to take on a big challenge to commemorate the event. Go big or go home, right? I was going to run 50 miles on my 50th birthday.

I kept training, slowly increasing my distances. I suffered some injuries. I tore my hamstring and then my meniscus. Recovery and getting back into my training were painful and frustrating.

I had a goal, and I was not going to quit. At least not while I still had a lot of time until my birthday. Time goes by. Work has to get done. Life interferes with the best of plans.

The fall before my birthday, I ran my first marathon. It was awesome and hard. I felt elated. I felt exhausted. I wanted to quit many times. I hurt. My knees had stabbing pain that subsided to a throbbing ache. I ignored the discomfort.

A quick aside here. The phrase "no pain, no gain" is one I do not like. If you're experiencing pain, then you need to stop and probably get medical attention. Seriously, do not work through your pain unless it is an emergency and your life or someone else's life depends on it. If it is discomfort, well, You Better Work! Work through discomfort and keep pushing back against it. Okay, back to my running journey.

I didn't go into it with a specific time I wanted to beat. I just wanted to go the distance. I allowed myself permission to walk when I needed to. I gave myself that space for recovery. I stopped at the aid stations. I rehydrated along the way.

At one point, the volunteers at the aid station gave out hydration gummies in paper cups. I got a chunk of frozen gummies from my first attempt. I may have forgotten to mention that this marathon was in November. It was a few degrees below freezing when it began and may have warmed to the upper 30s by the end.

So, there I am, running along, more shuffling along at this point, with a mouthful of frozen gummies. Okay, so this is happening, I remember thinking. I folded over the paper cup, put the rest of the gummies in my pocket for later, and kept on trucking. Over time, the frozen mass in my mouth thawed and then began to dissolve. It provided me with the hydration I needed, even though it was not what I had expected at first. The remaining gummies in my pocket warmed up and were refreshing when I ate them a few miles later.

Throughout the race, I talked negatively to myself. I should have trained more. I should have been more strict with my diet. I should have lost more weight. I should have done a lot of things, but it would be okay. Should have, would have, could have! Shut up and keep pushing!

Eventually, I completed my first marathon. I was confident I could do it, but crossing the finish line after 26.2 miles felt very good. I didn't run every step of the way. I did run most of it. I didn't come in first place. I did give it my very best on that day over that course. I achieved a new accomplishment. I was now a marathoner. I did it!

Then I relaxed. I didn't train as much. I didn't watch my diet as much.

But time didn't relax. My birthday was getting closer each day. It didn't care whether I ran or took another day off. Time didn't care whether I watched what I ate and fueled my body, or whether I enjoyed a bowl of ice cream. Time marched on from November to my birthday.

Two days before my 50th birthday, I had to make a decision. Was I really going to do this crazy thing? Was I really going to try to run 50 miles in a single day?

I hadn't trained as much as I should have. I had been training, but I could have done more. I hadn't slimmed down as much as I had planned to, though I was slimmer than I was for my marathon.

There was a long list of things I could have, should have, or would have done. It didn't matter anymore. The only thing that mattered was whether I would rise to the challenge or quit before I even tried.

The weather that day could not have been more ideal. The temperature was in the 60s, and it was sunny. No rain in the forecast. Only a slight breeze to keep things fresh.

I had a plan. I had a full hydro pack vest. I had snacks to eat along the way. I had a full charge on my phone and headphones. I had plotted out my course and knew what I was doing.

The first part of the run went very well. I got the hills out of the way and planned a refueling stop back at my car before heading out the other way. I reloaded my hydration pack vest, packed away some more GU gels and other quick-refueling snacks, and set out again. Twenty miles done and 30 more miles to go.

I kept the pace slow and steady. I hydrated and ate on schedule. I fought against the internal doubts. I fought against my body telling me to relax. I fought against the constant thought that I could just stop.

Nobody was making me do this. Nobody was going to be impressed that I had done this. I fought back with the only answer I had. I decided to do this, and I would be disappointed with myself if I allowed myself to quit. I would be so impressed if I could run for 50 miles on my 50th birthday! I was doing this for me, and I was going to do it, damn it!

I paused for a minute at the trail marker that marked my 50th kilometer. I was happy. If something happened and I couldn't finish, I had at least run 50 kilometers on my 50th birthday. That was an outstanding achievement. It just was not the one I set out to do.

I took a drink and ate a snack, then went back at it. Several miles further along, I met up with my girlfriend. Thirty-two miles complete and 18 more to go. The original plan had been for her to join me for a few miles for support, then drive ahead and meet me at the end.

She is a wonderful person and extremely determined. She is a seasoned runner and in good shape. She had not been in training for longer distances at that point. That did not stop her from staying right beside me until the end.

That run was one of the hardest things I have ever done in my life. I ran out of water. I ran out of snacks. I ran out of power for my headphones. I ran out of power for my phone. My watch even died. By the end, both she and I were nearly out of power as well. We were exhausted in every sense of the word.

It was dark, and we still had miles to go. I remember thinking I could just take a little break. There was a small hill next to the trail. If I could just sit down and lean back against it for a few minutes, I could get my energy back again.

At that point in the run, I remembered vividly what happened, or almost happened, on a training run about a month earlier. I was coming toward the end of a long run. The sun was nearly all the way down, so visibility was very low. I had just taken out my phone and turned on the flashlight feature. I was very happy I did. I quickly jumped to the right and ran past a snake that was warming itself on the trail. I am sure it wasn't poisonous, but still, I didn't want to bother him any more than he wanted to bother me.

All I kept thinking about was that it would be my luck to take a rest, sit on a poisonous snake, and get my butt bitten. I remember laughing a little at the thought. I shared with my girlfriend what I had found funny. All she said was that we were almost done, only a little more to go. Forty-seven miles done, and we had only three more miles until it was over.

Despite all the should-haves and should-not-haves, despite all the reasons I told myself as to why I should just quit, we crossed the finish line at 10:35 pm. I had done it. I had run 50 miles on my 50th birthday.

It took everything I had, as well as encouragement from one of the strongest people I have ever known. With her by my side, I was able to achieve this incredible achievement. Shout out to you, my muse, my precocious imp, my love. Thank you for staying by my side then and now. You are truly my partner. I love you, Kimberly.

Challenge yourself! You will discover a great deal about yourself. You will find that you can do amazing things. Push back against the forces trying to hold you in place.

Take control of where you are going with your life. Make your life what you want it to be.

It will take a lot of effort. It will take discipline. It will take persistence.

Know you CAN do it. You CAN get there. You WILL get there. You WILL achieve your goals. You will not give up. Now go get it!

Take on the challenge one bite at a time. Eat the elephant.

Take on the challenge.

What have you been thinking about doing but haven't taken the leap yet?__________________

What do you need to do before you can?______________________________

I will do it! Commit to yourself.

Signature:________________________

Chapter 9: You Time

Put time into yourself. Don't feel guilty about it. Make it your time.

I am going to go back to what I said back in Chapter 1: the only person you wake up with and go to bed with every day of your life is *you*. The only person you will always see in the mirror is *you*. *You* owe it to yourself to do as much as *you* possibly can to make yourself the best *you* that *you* can be.

You put time into maintaining your car. You make sure you buy clothes you like, and you replace them when they need to be replaced. You wash and iron them, so when you wear them, you look good. You keep your living area clean. Granted, some of us do better at it than others.

That is okay, too. We all have different standards that we judge to be right for us. You do you. Unless you aren't happy with this version of you, in which case it is time to work towards the version of you that you want to be. And here we are...

Put the time into you. There are only so many seconds in a day. You already have obligations you must meet. Outside of those things that absolutely must be done, such as going to work, you have some leeway in how you spend your time.

Some of you reading this are in the early phases of your military career. Thank you for stepping up to serve our country! Your time is already allocated to your strict military training schedule. Even with this, you have time you can choose to set aside for yourself.

You could learn or enhance your training in a form of martial arts, practice yoga (which is not easy), or engage in another activity focused on personal improvement. You could dive further into the topics of the previous chapters. Learn more about investing your money and managing your finances, and become a better communicator. There are many things to choose from. The important thing is that you commit to becoming the best version of *you* that *you* can be.

As you progress in your career, your schedule will become less regimented. You will have more freedom to choose how you spend your time. I encourage you to invest a part of your day in yourself. Do this each day. Do not let others infringe upon your *you* time. You give of yourself all of the hours of your day. Be stingy with the time you set aside for yourself.

For those of you not in the military, your time is still committed to your responsibilities. You have a certain amount of time it takes you to get up each day and get ready for work or school. It takes a certain amount of time for you to get to where you need to be. Once your work or school day is through, there are other things you need to do. It is daunting.

Parents have even more set commitments on their time. Children have to get to their appointments and be taken to and from school and after-school activities. They need help with their homework, and then they need to be settled into bed. Oh, yeah, maybe squeeze in some fun quality time with them along the way. Somehow, find the time to buy groceries, keep the house clean, do laundry, and prepare meals, as well as a myriad of other things that must be done along the way. Notice that I have not mentioned time for you to be with your spouse, partner, and friends. You need to make time for them as well, but heaven forbid we allow ourselves the room to think we should.

Yes, parents, you too must set aside *you* time. I know, with all the demands on your time, it feels impossible to even think about setting aside five minutes, let alone an hour for yourself. You may feel that it's just a dream.

But trust me—it isn't. If something is important to you, then you make time for it. *You* are important to *you*. You are the world to your family. You owe it to them and yourself to be the best person you can be.

You must be stingy with this time. It is so easy to take care of everything else and worry about yourself later. But guess what? Later rarely comes on its own. You have to turn later into now.

Trust me, those dishes will still be in the sink. Those floors will still need to be cleaned up in an hour. It is important that they are taken care of, but they are not central to everything else; YOU ARE.

Believe it or not, everything else in your world will adjust to this change in your schedule. Everything will get done. You *will* find a way to make this happen. Before you know it, this will be your new normal. You got this, whatever the *this* is.

You must push back against outside intrusions. You also, maybe even more so, need to push back against your inner intrusions. Reduce your distractions. Silence your self-doubt. You really do have this.

Change takes time and effort. There is a constant force that pushes back against change. It takes effort to change. It is natural to be tempted *just to stop* trying so hard. You do indeed deserve a break. It's even more true that you deserve to continually improve yourself.

It is easy to give in to that temptation to give up. But you deserve better. Those you love deserve better from you.

I came across a phrase a while ago about running: "The workout you are struggling with today will soon become your warmup."

The essence of this quote also applies to the changes you are making. Remember the reason you began reading this book? There is a reason you have read this far. You know you want to make a change. You know it won't be easy. And yet you have invested the time and effort to come this far in your journey with me. You are already making a change. Believe it or not, with reinforcement and your dedication, these changes you are making today will soon become your norm.

Take charge of your life. Make this commitment to yourself to become the best you that you can be. Keep pushing against the forces that try to hold you back or pull you back.

You are worth it, and you deserve it.

At the end of Chapter 7, you chose something to learn more about. At the end of Chapter 8, you chose something to challenge yourself with. Chapter 9 is all about keeping the you time set aside to do just that. Invest in yourself. Challenge yourself. Learn more about what you are interested in learning. This is your time. Make the most of it.

When is my you time?_________________

Where will I invest my you time? ___________

<u>Chapter 10: Conclusion</u>

Some common themes run throughout this book. First and foremost, you are the most important thing. I know the most important thing to you is the ones you love—your children, your spouse, your boyfriend or girlfriend, or your best friend.

It is good to have your focus outward. Think for a minute about how important you are to those people. I hope you see my point now. If you don't take care of yourself, you are not being the best you that you can be for them.

If you have an issue taking care of yourself because you feel selfish, vain, or something else silly, then do it for them. Be the best you that you can be, so you are the best person for them. Don't they deserve the best version of you? Well then, it is time to invest in yourself.

Each of these chapters has given you tools to invest in yourself. By being disciplined and dedicated, you can achieve the changes you want to make.

You *can* get yourself out of your challenging financial situation. Remember that you didn't get to this point overnight. It will take time to see the impact of your current choices. You will have to make the necessary corrections to get you to where you need to be. Keep making those small changes, and you will get there. Be disciplined. Be dedicated. Be persistent. Be the change. Believe.

Ask yourself, "Is this a want or is it a need?" It is okay to get the things you want, but make sure you satisfy the true needs before you entertain the wants.

Your investments need time to grow. As long as you continue to invest in them, they will keep doing their part and continue growing. You should have the beginnings of a plan. It is time to execute it.

Be brave! Do not invest in emotion. Invest based upon your analysis of the market and your research on the company or fund. Be brave when the stock market goes down. It will come back up. Stay steady and focus on why you decided to invest as you did. Avoid being impulsive.

To get your finances under control, you need to invest more in your needs than in your wants. Ensure that your needs are met so that you don't come to regret your wants. Don't risk your wants making you want to go back in time and do things differently.

We all spend time. We all spend money. But how often do we focus on investing in ourselves? When do we really focus on investing in our future? This is a much harder thing to do. It is not immediate, like spending money or time. That is right here in the present. We feel it. We have our hands around it.

Investing is more transcendent. It is something that we have to accept delayed gratification for. Humans are not good at delayed gratification. We want it, and we want it now.

Kind of sounds like a toddler, doesn't it? It's time to grow up. It's time to make your finances grow along with you. It's time to grow in your relationships as well.

You deserve love. You deserve a relationship that gives you as much as you put into it. You deserve a partner along this path of life. Be selective in who you choose to spend your time with. Be selective about whom you dedicate yourself to. Be all in once you find them. You deserve it. They deserve it from you.

Working on your communication skills takes effort. It is more than just talking. It is more than just listening. It takes an intentional effort to actively listen to what is being said. Focus on what is being communicated and try to avoid focusing on what you are going to say in response.

It is okay to take a beat after someone finishes speaking before responding. Your best response may be to ask for clarification of what they were saying. If you don't know, why not ask?

Once you know enough to respond, ensure you do so in response to what they said. Do not disregard what they said and jump to your point. That is not having a conversation. That is two people who are talking. The person to whom you are speaking might as well turn and talk to the wall.

Communicating is so very important. It matters in your professional life. It matters in your personal life. We all need to work on improving our communication skills.

Grow in the way you look at people, at the world in general. It's time to step back and take a longer view.

Go ahead, take a look around. You've got this. Take a breath. Take it all in. It has taken you a lot of effort to get where you are now. There have been ups and downs. You have learned valuable lessons along the way. You have achieved so much. Seriously, give yourself credit for what you have done. Now it is time to take it to the next level.

This book is only one part of it. I have done what I can to pass along some of the lessons I have learned.

You have taken a significant step by deciding to read this book. You also make a decision every time you choose to return to this book.

You have decided that you need to make a change. You need to do something different. You not only want things to be different, but you have also decided to take action. You kept coming back to it. You have demonstrated your determination for change. You are being disciplined.

Don't ever stop doing that!

Be the change you want. Keep evolving. Keep improving. Keep discovering. Continue working on becoming the best you that you can be.

Be disciplined.

Be dedicated.

Be persistent.

Be the change.

Believe in your plan.

Most of all, believe in you.

Resources

For more information on communication, I encourage you to go to HelpfulProfessor.com:

https://helpfulprofessor.com/communication-models/

The next place you can go is to Rest Less Co: https://restless.co.uk/health/healthy-mind/ways-to-improve-your-communication-skills/

I found the information from this blog post on BetterUp to be very informative and clear to understand: https://www.betterup.com/blog/effective-strategies-to-improve-your-communication-skills

This one goes into the relationship section as well. As you know, communication is central to any relationship:

https://psychcentral.com/blog/cultivating-contentment/2020/07/22-steps-to-better-communication-in-your-relationships#1

The list I found on Inspiringtips.com has some really good advice:

https://psychcentral.com/blog/cultivating-contentment/2020/07/22-steps-to-better-communication-in-your-relationships#1

This article on GoodHouseKeeping.com, "21 Signs of a Healthy Relationship, According to Therapists," is a very good read:

https://www.goodhousekeeping.com/life/relationships/g67951784/signs-you-are-in-a-healthy-relationship/

In Chapter 3, we discussed emotional intelligence. I did not go into much detail in the chapter. You can find much more information in this article on Psychologytoday.com provides a very good introduction to emotional intelligence, or EI for short:

https://www.psychologytoday.com/us/basics/emotional-intelligence?msockid=135275acf1fe608a205c6394f07261f6

This article on PsychCentral is full of really good information:

https://psychcentral.com/lib/what-is-emotional-intelligence-eq#examples

This article from Psychology.org is geared toward the workplace, but it can also be used for your personal interactions. People are really just people in the end. The environment may differ and influence their reactions, but basically, they/we are the same:

https://psychologyorg.com/culture-index-personality-types-survey-and-test/

Debt Management

Here is a great introduction to Debt Management from Nerd Wallet: https://youtu.be/F-mQRThLwUl

Another good article on Financestrategists.com: https://www.financestrategists.com/financial-advisor/debt-management/

Calculator.net has a great online calculator you can use to find out how to pay off your debt. You can plug in your own numbers to see how quickly you can pay it off by increasing your monthly payment. Alternatively, if you really need to decrease the amount you have been paying, you can see how long it will take to pay it back and, more importantly, how much it will cost you:

https://www.calculator.net/debt-payoff-calculator.html

Using a spreadsheet to track your debt is an excellent way to go. You can clearly see where you are and track your progress. You know the saying GIGO? Garbage in, garbage out. If you fudge your numbers, it will not help you. Be disciplined. Let it show you the ugly truth. Bring the bad out into the light of day:

https://www.thebalancemoney.com/free-debt-reduction-spreadsheets-1294284

How to pay off credit card debt:

https://www.thebalancemoney.com/pay-credit-card-debt-357427

The better you track where your money is going, the better you'll be able to decide how to get to where you want to be financially.

Investing

Okay, you have put in the work, and you are now at the point when you want to invest in your future. You want your money to get to work for you. Congratulations!!! That is a major achievement. Go ahead and pat yourself on the back. We covered some basics of investing. You can find more information from the following sources:

https://www.investor.gov/introduction-investing/investing-basics/investment-products/stocks

https://www.fool.com/investing/how-to-invest/?msockid=135275acf1fe608a205c6394f07261f6

https://www.investopedia.com/terms/c/certificateofdeposit.asp

https://www.fool.com/investing/how-to-invest/bonds/?msockid=135275acf1fe608a205c6394f07261f6

https://www.investopedia.com/investing-in-cryptocurrency-5215269

Never Stop Learning

https://www.herzing.edu/blog/benefits-lifelong-learning-how-continuously-develop-your-skills

https://online.jwu.edu/blog/lifelong-learning-what-it-is-and-why-it-matters/

https://hbr.org/2017/02/lifelong-learning-is-good-for-your-health-your-wallet-and-your-social-life

Challenge Yourself

https://inspiringtips.com/challenging-yourself/

https://pmc.ncbi.nlm.nih.gov/articles/PMC9891132/

https://www.psychologytoday.com/us/blog/strive-thrive/201408/how-greater-challenges-help-you-grow?msockid=135275acf1fe608a205c6394f07261f6

You Time

https://www.theplainsimplelife.com/time-is-important/

https://www.psychologytoday.com/us/blog/automatic-you/202302/people-make-time-for-what-they-want-rightfully-so?msockid=135275acf1fe608a205c6394f07261f6

Final Words

I hope you take the opportunity to visit some of the sites in the previous section. They have a wealth of information on each of them. Continue your learning. Dive deeper into the topics. At the end of the day, know that you've got this. You can get to where you want to be. It will not be easy, but I believe in you!

I wrote this book to share the lessons I have learned along my life path. I am happy you have read them. Thank you for taking this journey with me. I hope I have taught you some things that will help you.

If you know someone who would benefit from reading this book and the lessons I have shared with you, let them know why they should read it.

If you want to stay in touch, you can reach out to me on my website https://tlscottauthor.com or email me at TLScottauthor@tlscottauthor.com.

Reviews are very important for authors. Please take a moment to let the world know what you thought of *Things I Wish I Knew When I Stood Where You Are Now* at either http://www.Goodreads.com or the site you bought the book from.

I look forward to hearing from you.

All the best,

T. L. Scott

October 2025

About the Author

T. L. Scott is a Navy retiree with over 24 years of service. He has a bachelor's degree in Business Management and a master's degree in Transformational Leadership. He is the author of five fiction novels as well as the children's picture book series *A Scary Story*.

He currently splits his time between Michigan and Virginia with his partner and their two cats.

https://tlscottauthor.com